Urney - History / People / Place

Carmel Quigley (Clady Woman!)

URNEY

HISTORY PEOPLE PLACE

Web Site: www.urney.info

E-Mail: daniel@urney.info
john@urney.info
brid@urney.info

Web Site: www.doneyloopyouthclub.com
E-Mail: bridmcgrenra@yahoo.com

ISBN 978-0-9568891-0-2
Published By Doneyloop Youth Club Ltd
Front cover photos by Paul Mc Crory.
Back cover Clady Bridge© by Jim Hamilton.
Front inside cover York Dairy by Mary Mc Corkell.
Printed by Browne Printers Ltd., Letterkenny

Contents

3.	Introduction	146.	Our Country
5.	Foreword	147.	The Ballad Of Bella Brooks
6.	Foreword	149.	Urney Oats
7.	Urney Poem	150.	The Hunterstown Ghost
8.	Settlers, Sorcerers, Saints, Scholars And Soldiers	151.	Clady C1912
		155.	The Magherycallaghan Ghost
17.	Antiquity	157.	William Burke
21.	"Landscape Shapes Culture"	160.	Honest John Kelly
31.	Maps Of The Manor Of Castlefinn	161.	Tobias Mullen
42.	The Field	162.	Master Robert
43.	Early Names In Urney	165.	Rogans of Glentown, urney
44.	The Great Hunger	172.	Castlefinn G.A.A.
45.	The World At War	179.	Castlefinn Celtic
48.	Urney's World War One Dead	183.	Urney St Columba's
50.	A Nation Divided	198.	Clady Strollers
53.	A Glimpse At The Parish Of Urney	200.	Doneyloop Youth Club
65.	Urney Bell	203.	Michael (Mac) Mclaughlin
68.	Alt Presbyterian Church	205.	Christina Speers
72.	Renovation At Alt Presbyterian Church 1990	207.	Joe Mc Devitt
		210.	And Mary Got The Blame
74.	Christ Church, Urney	211.	Shopping In Alt.
89.	Urney Presbyterian Church	212.	Taking The Tea
94.	Farming, From Tenant To Landlord	213.	The Show Fire
		214.	Forts And Fairies
99.	Urney Chocolates, Sweet Success	216.	Bibliography
106.	Flax Mills		
119.	Fair Day		
121.	The Grand River Finn		
125.	Roads And Bridges Of Urney		
127.	The Wee Donegal		
135.	Landlords		
136.	Urney Players		
140.	School Days In Urney		

INTRODUCTION

"There is no want of material for local history if all sources could be tapped"

These were the words of Fr. Walter Hegarty in 1933 on his rambles around Urney. When we started this 'idea' way back in October 2009, little did we know how long and hard it would be. As Fr. Hegarty wrote" there is no want of material". All you have to do is find it! And so a meeting was organized by Doneyloop Youth club for the local people to bring what local history they had to us, whether in song or story handed down, a yarn or in print. We have looked at many documents of historical value to the Clady and Doneyloop area and as far as practical, have left the names of people and townlands as they were spelt in the documents. Many other documents and photos of great value have been loaned to us by many people.

We are indebted to the following people for the help and encouragement they have brought to this book. Firstly, to the authors for your time and commitment, I know what you went through! To Joe Mc Devitt, Thomas Bogle, Brian Donnelly, Bernie Mc Corkell, Paddy Mc Gee, Cyril Mc Gee, Nancy Mc Gee, Jackie Langan, Joe Hunter, Ursula O' Faodhagain, Jim and Isobel Roulston, Mac Mc Loughlin, Breda Mc Connell, Bettie Nelis, Jane Domitric, Joe Mc Glinchey, Patsy Mc Ginley, Thomas Henderson, Terence and Dorothy Mc Kinlay, Dr. Kay Muhr, Dónall Mac Giolla Easpaig, Rev. Raymond McKnight, Fr. Brian Mc Goldrick, Fr. Phillip Donnelly, Fr. Kieran Devlin, Priscilla Mc Kinney, Rev John Honeyford, Sam Bogle, Ryan O' Neill, Ann Speers-Crooks, Cecil Darragh, David Darragh, Dermot and Theresa Kelly, Bill Mc Cauley, Hugo Mc Corkell, Mrs O' Flaherty, Daniel Crawford, Jim Hamilton, Paul Mc Crory, Augustine Coyle, Laurence Holland, Brendan Molloy, John Molloy and Ivan Knox. THANK YOU.

To Celia Byrne and Allison Bell for all the typing sometimes at short notice! And to the emergency typing crew of Aoife and Clíodhna Mc Menamin for when things were getting tight! To John Byrne for his technical expertise, to Kathy Mc Menamin, Margaret Mc Menamin, Jason Harold, Brid Mc Grenra and Mary Mc Menamin for proof reading and to the staff of the Strabane, Omagh, Letterkenny, and Ballybofey Libraries, The Public Records Office of Northern Ireland and the National Archives Dublin.

We also want to thank our sponsors, The Donegal C.D.B Peace and Reconciliation partnership without whom this book would not have been possible and finally to you, we present this book as a small reminder of where your people have come from ,their joy and happiness, heartache and hardship. We have only scratched the surface of Urney History. There is more to be found, and to repeat the wish of Fr. Hegarty, we hope someday another generation will uncover just a little bit more of our Urney past.

For and on behalf of Doneyloop Youth Club,

Vice Chairman,

Daniel Mc Menamin.

Project supported by PEACE III Programme managed for the Special EU Programmes Body by Donegal County Council

Foreword
Urney History People Place

Could any title more encapsulate and capture the sense of identity and belonging that an appreciation of the past can mean to the present and future generations as in a small community such as Urney? I would contend that because it has often been suggested that all history is local a community without its history is akin to a man without a memory. So it is vitally important that historical memory is consigned to the record.

Unlike so many blessed with local knowledge who sadly shirk this challenge Daniel Mc Menamin seeks to address that void and with this excellent and all embracing production has done his community invaluable service. It is our privilege and, I would suggest, our duty to gather with pious care what knowledge remains and to hand it onto the unborn generations. One often hears vague and sketchy statements about some event that has happened even within living memory but more often than not that never gets recorded and is consigned to oblivion. Many of the old ruins that speak of flight or foray, of culture or religion are crumbling and their story is fading from the minds of our contemporaries. And their past glory fades with them.

In reality it is the small incidents of the past that interests one profoundly, more especially if they bear on our own life and that of our local community. A community can regenerate itself and a production such as this can be the perfect vehicle to do so and I add my personal congratulations and that of the Co Donegal Historical Society to the author and his like minded contemporaries of willing this valuable all inclusive legacy to the community of Urney.

Col. Declan O Carroll (retd)
President
Co Donegal Historical Society

March 2011.

Foreword

Urney History People Place

I am very grateful for the invitation to contribute a foreword to the publication of the "Urney" book.

To produce a book such as this is a most onerous and painstaking undertaking and all those involved have my admiration and congratulations on the finished product.
It is without doubt the contributors to this local history book have done us all a great service and to the community of Urney, given them an insight into their areas rich and colourful history.

The area covered within the pages of the book is a wide one indeed and embraces many aspects of the history of the wider Urney area, the people who have lived there, the hardships they have faced, overcome and conquered. A lesson for us all in these trying times.

As well as being a most interesting read, it is both educational and informative and should recommend itself to those interested in history and family history as well as the wider local community.

I would recommend this book as a most enjoyable read and well worth the time to do so.

Hugh B
McGarrigle

Strabane Family
History Society

URNEY

"Tall Croghan looks down on the meadows
That be by the fords of the Finn
And many a rich beaming Valley
Which the sword of the spoiler did win."
By William Collins

Urney - History / People / Place

Settlers, Sorcerers, Saints, Scholars and Soldiers

By Damien Hunter

The Parish of Urney and Castlefin would have resembled most, if not all Irish parishes in the early Christian period. Pagan Ireland's rich and imaginative mythological history was communicated orally by the bards down through the generations until St Brigid and St Columba founded convents and monasteries. The advent of Christianity with St Patrick was accompanied with the development of the Irish alphabet and written word along Latin lines. This witnessed the growth of literature affected by the earlier Celtic druids notions of the 'Otherworld' and the Catholic ideas of the 'Afterlife'.

As such the early Christian period would have been characterised by the Celt's emotional swings between dream and reality, his aspirations and experiences and his sense of bad Gods versus good God. In short, his pagan amorality was being displaced with a new Christian morality as the 'graceful' formalities of a new society were imposed on the wild passions of the old society. This meant that the native romanticism of the pagan Celt as found in his myths, legends and histories would be coloured by the 'literate druids' or monks. Their censured versions of the pagan myths and legends (as recorded and preserved in the monastic transcripts) were more in tune with the tradition of foreign classicism. The humble Irish monk preserved all the classical learning of Western Europe, by copying Greco-Roman and Judeo-Christian literature after the Barbarians destruction of Rome around 475A.D. More importantly as Kenneth Clark said;

"Looking back from the great antiquities of 12th C France or 17th C Rome, it is hard to believe that for quite a long time almost a hundred years, western Christianity survived by clinging to places like Skellig Michael, a pinnacle of rock eighteen miles from the Irish coast rising 700 feet out of the sea".

Urney monastery too, may have played its part in the preservation of civilization, who knows? There is a reference to Urney parish in the Book of Kells. A lot of learning that was preserved in all the monasteries throughout Ireland has been lost to pirates, pillagers' and plunderers. A lot of historical records concerning the Strabane area have also been lost due to the bombing of Strabane Town Hall in 1972, whereby all papers and records tracing the origins and evolution of the locality are now gone forever.

Most of what follows in this chapter is conjecture and extrapolation on what is known from the early Christian and medieval periods in others areas of Ireland.

The 12th Century 'Book of Invasions' records that Ireland is believed to have been subjected to six invasions from different ethnic groups: namely, (1)Cessair, (2)Partholón, (3)Nemed, (4)the Fir Bolg, (5)the Túatha Dé Dannan and (6)the sons of Mil Espáne (the Milesians). Regardless of the book's historical accuracy being challenged by modern day revisionist historians, it is most likely that the Milesians, the first Gaelic settlers of Ireland were among the latest settlers of the parish of Urney and Castlefin, around 500 – 350 BC. Evidence of this settlement is found at Urney Fort located on a low hill overlooking the River Finn. Professor Brian Scott dated its construction as being in the Iron Age, around 500 BC[1].

There is a monument on the top of Croaghan Hill testifying that Íth, King of the Mlesians is buried there; hence the name MagnÍtha (the Finn Valley).

A reckless warrior race, the Celts were described by Vendyres as being a;

"free independent and impetuous people, drunk on war and victory (full of) the joy of adventure even in the land of fairies a sense of marvel felt in the chronicles penned by the monks in the silence of the convent; for even in the holy legends and lives of the saints one hears an echo of it, giving us a hagiography so different to that of the continent."[2]

A view of Croaghan hill from Skelpy

The Celts had sacked Rome only forty years earlier in 390 BC. Their military might was attributable to their being highly skilled metal workers and the sense of pride that this bestowed upon them probably accounts for their free - spiritedness and a haughty – minded sense of individualism.

Pre – Christian Celtic Ireland was constituted by five parts called 'cuígí' (provinces), of which were further sub-divided into smaller statelets or 'tuatha.' In total, there would have been a hundred and fifty tuatha throughout Ireland at this time. Each tuatha had a stratified class system presided over by a warrior class headed by a king, supported by a priestly class (druids) that legitimised their power and the bards who eulogized their heroic deeds. This early dynastic society was aristocratic, regional, local and personal; and explains why the Irish were incapable of becoming a politically united nation for another fifteen hundred years. Whilst a common ancestral memory equipped the Irish mind with a sentimental sense of 'racial oneness' due to a shared language and culture, it equally insisted on a 'regional otherness' and an identity rooted in locality. Local loyalties were forged by a personal identity of belonging to the tribe. Blood and place accounted for the amount of internecine warfare that would characterise the Irish for centuries and make Machiavelli's medieval Italy look civilized in comparison with its contemporaneous Irish conflicts and tales of ancient Irish battles.

Early Irish tales have been classified into four groups:

(a) The Mythological Cycle, whose main protagonists were the Side (the Fairies), who dwelled among the burial mounds of Knowth, Dowth and New Grange

(b) The Ulster Cycle, which describes the exploits of the Ulaid.

(c) The Kings Cycle, which traces the activities of the 'historical' King, and

(d) The Finn Cycle which details the adventures of Finn MacCool and his Fianna.

The imaginative richness of the tales hailed from its main motifs of changelings, changing seasons, love, animals, the open air, the hunt and food and drink. These came from an early Irish shorthand for debauchery, partying, running off with other men's women, cattle rustling and bloodletting. All of this was an oral history as the Druids distrusted the written word. However for a pagan people the Celts mythology and belief systems were dominated by the notion of the supernatural 'Otherworld'. Man created the Gods in the image of himself, as the Kings were celebrated as sacral – deified as demi–gods by the bards in poetry, story and song – by being married to the tribal goddesses. This now was supported by the druids or sorcerers who "...were at once the priests, the physicians, the diviners, the theologians, the scientists and the historians of their tribes. All spiritual power, all human knowledge were invested in them..." [3]

They literally had the power over life and death. They made sacrificial bonfires of human beings encased in huge figures of wicker – work to Lugh Lamfada, the Gaelic sun-god.

J.R. Walsh traces the earliest surviving written linkage of Saint Patrick with the present day Diocese of Derry as being found in the 7th Century 'Brevarium' (Brief Account') by Bishop Tirechán, who noted that Patrick travelled over the" Gap of the Sons of Conall' (Barnesmore Gap) to Mag Íth (Mag n Ítha or the Finn Valley) to found a great Church called Donaghmore in the west of what is now the diocese.[4]

St Patrick's Church of Ireland Donaghmore believed to on the site of the church founded by St Patrick.

The arrival of Saint Patrick with his suitcase of Christianity ended the power of the druids and their 'Gods' forever. At a historical convention in Raphoe in 2006, Mary Harte presented a paper claiming that Saint Patrick crossed the River Finn at Cladyford (Just north of Clady Bridge) en route for his confrontation with the druids at Raphoe's Stone Circle. The main weapon in his armoury being, he had found a way of plummeting the depths of the Irish mind through a transformation that made it more humane and noble, yet keeping it distinctly Irish. He substituted the Irish Red Martyrdom of a glorious death on the battlefield with a Green Martyrdom that consisted of a 'magic' that came from the hand of a good God who did not demand human sacrifices, as Christ had died once for all, the scriptures and the hagiography of classical literature. Saint Patrick's introduction of the figure of the martyred saint as proof of the redemptive power that Christianity offered its followers stole the show from the druids. By choosing the tuatha as the unit of ecclesiastical jurisdiction, for selling his ideas, he personalised and localised the saints as local heroes whose "miracles added to the prestige and power of a territory, community and extended family. Intercessors and mediators, saints bridged the gap between the sacred and the profane, the dead and the living, the familiar and the unknown".[5] Saint Patrick transformed the pagan Kings into mortal heroes and replaced them with new demi–gods – the saints

Our local hero would prove to be Saint Columba (Colmcille), who "belonged to the royal dynasty in north western Ireland known as Cenél Conaill claimed, along with several other important dynasties, to be descended from the legendary high – king known as Niall of the Nine Hostages. All of these related dynasties were collectively known as the Uí Néill, literally 'the descendants of Niall'. For most of the second half of the first Christian millennium, the Uí Néill were among the most powerful people in Ireland and shared between themselves the significant, sacred high – kingship of Tara."[6] Columba is believed to have founded Derry monastery in 535. Local folklore has it that he had founded Urney monastery as part of his familia (confederation of churches) in the mid – 6th Century. This now would be supported by Walsh who states "there was a convent founded by Cognat in the parish of Urney. Samthann of Colbroney in County Longford (d 739), a nun revered as a spiritual director, was a novice with Cognat's community."[7] Folklore also has it Saint Adomnán was born at the foot of Croaghan Hill. He was the biographer of Saint Columba's 'Vita Columbae' (life of Columba) circa 697 which detailed Columba's prophecies, angelic visions and miracles. One such miracle concerned Columba separating a demon from a spring worshipped by the Picts as a god. While the Greeks had viewed springs as the "fountains of the nymphs," the Celtic Irish equivalents were Holy wells. It is possible Saint Bridget's well in Cormakilly was brought into the Christian traditions as part of a similar miracle being performed by her. Whilst there are no ways of establishing these tales as historical facts, similarly, there are no ways of disproving them either.

Undoubtedly Saint Columba's royal blood and connections helped him propagate Christianity through his missionary zeal that consisted of prayers, peregrinations, penances and pilgrimages. This model of monasticism so flourished that it replaced the diocese as the ecclesiastical mode of organisation and administration altogether by the 8th Century, as all members of the tuatha became the spiritual subjects of the Abbots.

Father Donnelly provides a fascinating depiction of what monastic life would have been like in Ardstraw monastery although not laying any claims to any angelic visions; he envisions it as being mainly constituted by a church, a separate sacristy and a cemetery. There was besides a refectory for the community a guest house for visitors or pilgrims and would have resembled a small town. "The monks were for the Christian people their preachers, teachers and spiritual directors. Intellectual work held an honourable place. Some brothers wrote poetry and studied Holy Scripture, theology and profane literature. At the beginning of the 6th Century the native Irish tradition of learning had become suspect as pagan. By the early decades of the 6th Century, however, we find the great Colmcille (Columba) is taking lessons which are representative of the old learning. The majority of the poets are now Christian.

The union of the two cultures, Pagan and Christian began about the year 600. The clergy and monks displaced the druids as the learned men, the philosophers and theologians of the nation. The scribes devoted time to the transcription of books with pen and ink on vellum.[8] What really happened was this new Irish literati (the scribes) had sanitized the old pagan tales altogether. Well almost.

Some old habits die hard. A sympathetic scribe concocted an imaginary meeting between Óisín and Saint Patrick in a series of spirited ballads. Óisín one of the great mythological heroes returning to earth from Tír na nóg (land of the young) after a few hundred years, bemoans the departure of the pagan world and the arrival of Christianity. What, he says "is the use to him of eternal life where there is no hunting, or wooing fair women, or listening to the songs and tales of the bards?"[9] In Óisín's eyes (or the scribe's?) Saint Patrick had killed the craic – a real party pooper! Óisín should have hung around for another few hundred years.

The old pagan traits soon returned...."The conquest by Cenél nEógain of the territory of Mag n Ítha, the valley of the River Finn in Donegal..." ushered blood-letting back into the parish of Urney, with their defeat of Cenél Conaill. The Annals of Ulster record fighting between the two dynasties in Mag n Ítha in 732, 733 and 734 fighting in which Cenél Conaill was on the losing side. The kingdom may however have passed back to Conél after the death of Aéd Allán of Cenél n Eógain in 743, for Cenél Conaill appears to have been defending it when it was conclusively defeated in 789 at Clótech (or Clady)."[10] [So, there you have it: the Tyrone and Donegal men were at it even then. Thank God, it's only over Gaelic matches these days.]

But, it didn't end there. By 1179, the O' Carolans and the people of the Lifford area were blood-letting with the Mohens and the O' Gormleys of Urney. "They concluded their peace in the hallowed church of Ardstraw, swearing oaths on the relics of that church and those of Donaghmore and Urney. On the following day Auliffe O' Gormley repaired to the house of O'Carolan to demand further guarantees. He was killed in the middle of the meeting in the doorway of the house with three of his people, in the presence of his own sister, the wife of Donagh (O' Carolan)." [11]

By April 1689, everything was hunky-dory again. The O' Neills and the O. Donnells, the O' Carolans and the O' Gormleys were all united again to face a new breed of settler. On 16th April 1689 the Jacobite forces under the ousted King James II were on their way to Wililamette Derry. Coming from Newtonstewart "James rode on by a sunken road in Mulvin Bog, to Clady Fort. Near Clady is a hill called Sneezing Hill were it is believed that James sneezed, this being a good omen. The crossings on the Finn were held for a short period by Protestant forces who then fell back on Derry, where the siege began on April 21." [12] This was the first battle regarding the siege of Derry and it happened at Cladyford. It is commemorated on a plaque in St. Columba's Cathedral, Derry.

The introduction of the Penal Laws in 1695 had serious implications for the state of health of Catholicism and Presbyterianism (which was also outlawed). The Catholics clung to Mass Rocks to celebrate the sacraments and preserve the Faith; one such Rock would have been located in Skelpy Glen. Father Donnelly states:"popular memory recalls the killing of a priest at Fern Hill three miles north of Castlederg the body was carried on a litter of willow staves and buried near a well on land now held by John Barron, in the townland of Drumdoit, seventy yards from the border at the appropriately named Priestsessiagh. Later the willow rods, which had been thrown into the grave, took root and it is believed became two trees." [13] It is more likely that this priest was killed by the 'Redcoats' or 'Head hunters' on his way to or from the Mass Rock at Skelpy. Another priest's body was found at a narrow glen on the western side of the Kilclean road, one mile north of Castlederg. The priests' names were believed to be a Father Ward and a Father Gallagher, thus they would have been carrying on the tradition of saintly martyrlogy in the history of the Irish Church, as Cromwell had St Oliver Plunkett murdered earlier at Drogheda in 1649.

By 1766, what is believed to be the first Catholic Seminary in the Diocese of Derry was founded by Father Philip Mc Devitt who came home to his diocese from Paris, where he was Doctor of the Sorbonne, and was ordained bishop in 1766. Persecution drove him from the Moville district to Clady on the banks of the Finn, in the Parish of Urney. Finally, about 1780 Bishop Mc Devitt moved to Derry, the first bishop to reside there for 180 years, since the death in 1601 of Redmond Ó Gallagher. [14]

This evidenced a growing French influence on the Catholic Church in Ireland after the 1789 French Revolution. Maynooth was founded by the British Government in 1795 to purchase the Catholic Church's loyalty and this mind set would soon filter down to local level in the Parish of Urney. Many French refugee professors cultivated a spirit of 'Gallicism' among the Irish clergy by inculcating the notions that one, the Church must be loyal to the British Throne and two, that in matters of morals they should be responsible for the management of the Irish people's conscience and consciousness. When the United Irishmen were founded by the Presbyterians in 1791 with the aim of uniting 'Protestant, Catholic and Dissenter' they were, horror of all horrors, influenced by the social, political and religious principles of revolutionary France. Just before the 1798 Rebellion, in June of that year, the local parish priest Arthur Mc Hugh, had furnished a representative of the Duke of Abercorn with a letter containing hundreds of parishioners signatures declaring their support for the Crown. This reflects a growing concern at the hierarchy of the Catholic Church that Catholics would depart en masse from the Church by converting to Presbyterianism and the principles of 'Liberty, Equality and Fraternity' which had been responsible for the butchering of thousands of priests during the 1789 French Revolution.

It also reflects that the parishioners could have pulled a sneaky one by getting themselves off the British Intelligence suspect lists by not admitting that they were members of a Secret Society. Imagine! At the 'Derg Bridge Fair' of that year a spy for the Duke of Abercorn reported "that it was unusual to see so many people leaving the festivities sober and declared that this was a sign of the evidence of United Irishmen who would not drink for fear of passing on valuable information."[15] So there you have it; you're dammed if you do drink and dammed if you don't! It would be fair to say this wasn't an intelligence system of MI5 proportions but it would have been most likely that the Catholics hadn't the money to drink and the Presbyterians hadn't the pre-disposition to drink. Everybody knows the Presbyterians are more death on the drink than the 'Pioneers' and would have made up a legion of Father Matthews'. Ossian would have been broken-hearted.

In 1795, a sectarian clash between the 'Catholic Defenders' and the 'Hedge Masons' was recorded as "six people were killed in a scuffle in Castlefinn". The moral of the story being you don't mess with the Castlefinn boys. Ossian would have been delighted.

The age old Celtic tradition of atavistic individualism appears to make all Irishman no respecters of any laws at all, and explains why the Irish keep reverting to their old ways, emotionally oscillating between dream and reality, and Pagan amorality and Christian morality.

No wonder RG Collingwood wrote;

"History proper is the history of thought.

There are no mere events in history"

References

1. McNulty pp1-8
2. Quoted in O'Faolain, pp30-31
3. 2. Squire, p34
4. Jefferies and Devlin, pp33-34
5. 4. Nagy, ppvii-viii
6. Jefferies and Devlin, pp20-21
7. Do p44
8. Father Donnelly pp8-10
9. Squire, p226
10. Bartlett and Jeffery, pp28-29
11. Donelly, p15
12. Do. P59
13. Do. P75
14. Do. P65
15. Mc Nulty p20

Antiquity

By Ellen Byrne

Ring-Forts

Ring-Forts are areas of land enclosed by one or more earthen banks/ditches. People lived in Ring-Forts up to the twelfth century. These forts were built by digging a ditch using the earth and stone to form a circular bank. A timber or wattle fence was constructed on the bank. Inside the ring, one or two houses were built. They had timber frames, wattle-and-daub walls, thatched roofs and a hearth in the centre of the floor. Smaller buildings in the ring-fort were used for storing food or for providing shelter to animals. These were for centuries after the 1200s believed to be "fairy forts", home to fairies and never interfered with by farmers, in spite of the years they lay uninhabited. Even now it is rare for a farmer to damage or remove a fairy fort or anything growing on it, though many will vehemently deny believing in fairies!

Ring-Forts in the Urney area included Urney fort, Scotstown, Gortkilly, Drumdoit, Doneyloop, Clady, Lisdoo, Cavannaweery, Cloghfin and Halftown. The fort in Clady is believed to have been where 'the Grove' now stands and is mentioned in 972 A.D., with the 'Black fort 'of Lisdoo lost to history. Sadly only Drumdoit and Urney fort remain today. . Excavations by students from Strabane Grammar School in 1970 tell us that the internal diameter of the Urney fort is 173ft and that the fort had internal and external stone facing. Mr. Brian Scott, Dept of Archaeology, Queens University Belfast who was part of the excavation team states "The internal stone facing is stepped in two areas, with a platform ca. 2ft wide running between the upper and lower steps. It is fairly certain that this platform ran the whole way round the interior of the fort."

Souterrains were built under some of the houses. These were underground passages/tunnels that went under the earthen bank that led outside the ring-fort. This feature was present in the ring-forts found in Drumdoit and Scotstown. Archaeologists believe that souterrains were used for storing food because they were cool, and as hiding places or escape passages when the ring-fort was attacked. The forts were lived in by farmers and their families, who needed the earthen bank and ditch to protect them from wild animals and from attacks by other families.

Standing Stones

A Standing Stone refers to single upright stone, usually located on their own. Other names for Standing Stones are; Coirthe, Dallán, Gallán, Lia, Liagán, Monolith, Menhir, Pillarstone, Stollaire. Some of them were placed to mark important burials; others were placed to mark important borders of territories or farmsteads and others still for travelled routes. Most standing stones date from the Bronze Age but some are much earlier, Neolithic, although some standing stones were erected in the 18th or 19th century as scratching posts for cattle. Tall stones were placed in circles or in rows or stood by themselves. Some of the single standing stones are very likely the last stone of a portal tomb to survive. A few might even be a sole survivor of a stone circle or row. Pairs of stones also occur of which one may be pointed or rounded and the other flattened or grooved, suggesting male and female. Some farmers believed in driving their cattle between the standing stone pair to encourage fertility.

The entrance to the stone circles is usually in the north-east of the circle, and the smallest stone in the circle is opposite the entrance. According to the Archaeological Survey of County Donegal (1983), the summit of Fearn hill is home to a stone circle surviving to a height of .2 metres. The stone rows are also set in a north-east/south-west direction. Archaeologists believe this is linked to the movements of the sun. When ogam writing was introduced to Ireland from Wales, before Christianity had arrived some long standing stones were used for inscriptions, usually memorials of named people. These stone monuments may have been used as part of some religious ceremony, as well as for burials.

Standing stones used to be found in Coolyslin, Lisdoo, Fern and Skelpy, with one that seems to be more recent still standing in Glentown. The Ordinance Survey Memoirs of Urney,1836 states "In the townland of Upper Alt, close to the east side of the road from Castlefin to Castlederg and about 3 miles from the former place, are some remarkable stones bearing the appearance of antiquity and called the Giant's Grave. The stones are 5 in number, 3 standing and 2 fallen. The largest standing stone is 5 feet high and seem such about 1 foot in the ground. The 2 fallen are each 6 feet in length about 4 feet broad and 2 feet thick." Sadly the Giant's Grave, like a lot of the other Antiquities can no longer be seen in Urney.

A view of Drumdoit fort

Stone Monuments of a gone-by age as told by Leila Patterson, 1936/37.

"The locality of Castlefin has many old stones and rocks. Long before the time of the Red Branch Knights the Finn Valley was known as the Laggan Valley, but now it is called the Finn Valley in memory of the great hero Finn Mc Cool who lived in this valley. In many places the old name Laggan Valley is still retained. Finn was born in Glenfinn, according to the legend Finn Mc Cool was buried at Barrick Rocks in the locality of Castlefin. On top of this grave stand upright stones in memory of him. Close by to this grave is a Saints grave on the side of a hill at Barrick Rocks and it is covered with much the same kind of stones.

According to legend there lived at Croghan two giants one of whom was Finn Mc Cool. They held a competition to see which one could fire a rock the longest distance and Finn won. While the rock was in flight it broke, one half fell at Cormackelly* and the other half fell at Lios Doo at Clady. Finn also threw a rock from Croghan and it fell in the river Finn.

At Stranamuck in Mr. Nelson's field there is a tree standing. There is supposed to be a giant buried in under this tree. Close by to this tree stands a stone with indecipherable writing on it.

Outside the district of Castlefin at Drumdoit* here is a holy well. This well was blessed by Saint Brigit in days gone by. The Catholics come here from far and near to be cured. Some leave medals and others leave broaches in remembrance of their visits. There is a stone nearby on which the people worshipped their God during the period of Penal Laws. Long ago this stone was further up the field, but Father Hegarty of Clady lifted this stone and placed it at the well. It still lies there to the present day."

Leila Patterson.

*Leila Seems to have mixed the townland's up with the rock landing in Drumdoit not Cormakilly, and the well is in Cormakilly not Drumdoit. Finn Mc Cool's rock is now buried beside St Safan's National School, the top of which can still be seen. Locals tell of Finn's hand print which could be seen on the rock.

"Landscape shapes culture"

By Daniel Mc Menamin

The townland is a unique feature of the Irish landscape with over 62,000 townlands throughout Ireland. The townland or bally (Baile, Ballyboe) is the smallest officially-defined geographical division of land. Many townlands pre-date the Norman invasion (1169) with the majority of names being of Gaelic origin.

Land divisions once used in the Urney area include,

Ballybetagh – at one stage the largest measure of land generally containing four quarters

Quarter – generally contained three ballyboes

Ballyboe – a townland which normally contains three Sessiaghs.

Sessiagh – 1/3 of a townland.

Tullagh – a Ballyboe and a Sessiagh.

The majority of townlands on the Donegal side of Urney have retained their original name. Some Sessiaghs have become townlands, new townlands have been formed and a few townlands have changed names. Urney on the Tyrone side has not been as fortunate with some of the biggest changes of townland names in Ulster. Most of these changes happened in the one quarter of Church land (four ballyboes) leased to Mathew Babbington (1654). The four ballyboes, Aghenedawnagh, Cogan, Nurnin and Longford no longer exist but are believed to take in 14 modern townlands of which only four have Irish names, Urney, Inchenny, Clady and Carrickone. Some of the rest of the townlands are believed to have taken their names from plantation tenants.

One of our 'lost areas of land' was a place called Bellim'leer on the Map of Strabane Barony, 1609 and called Balli McClary on the William Petty map of Tyrone, 1672. This area was not by the way part of the Church lands but is believed to have included one or all of the fallowing, Doneygowen, Lisdoo, Hunterstown and Skerryglass, all of these townlands been west of the Clady burn. The Quarter of Drumbane (Donegal) was also known as Ballymaclier (See Drumbane). Balli McClary, Bellim'leer (Tyrone) and Ballymaclier (Donegal) must have been the same place? With the Tyrone/Donegal boundary only set in 1585 it is possible that the four townlands in Tyrone were once part of the Quarter of Drumbane.

Townlands used to have small villages connected to them made up of the farm house of the tenant farmer and several cottages/cabins which contained the farm labourers, cottiers and their families. If your family was associated with the area before the famine, it is likely they lived and farmed from one of those Villages.

ALT LOWER - AN TALLT ÍOCHTARACH – The lower Glen

Alt lower contains one hundred and eighty four acres. Villages in the area included Alt lower and Kennan's town.

ALT UPPER - AN TALLT UACHTARACH – the Upper Glen

Alt Upper contains six hundred and sixteen acres and was part of the glebe lands of Donaghmore parish. Alt Upper had at one stage several lime stone quarries and lime kilns and one kiln has survived intact to this day. Villages in the area included Alt Upper, Alt Mountain and Barleyhill.

BALLYLAST – AN BAILE LOISCTHE – The Burnt Townland

The name "An Baile Loiscthe" is believed to have originated from the burning of land to make it more fertile. Ballylast contains one hundred and fifty five acres. Villages - Ballylast and Ballylast Upper.

BELLSPARK (CHURCH LAND, 1654) – Eng. Bell, a surname

Bellspark is one of our townlands in the Urney area connected to the church lands leased to Mathew Babbington, the Bells presumably been the tenants. The word "Park" was introduced by the Anglo-Normans and connotes simply a 'field' or 'pasture'. Bellspark contains seventy acres.

CALHAME – COLD HOME – Sc. Cal hame.

Calhame is a Scottish word meaning "cold home", which seems to have been used to donate land not having the advantage of much sunlight. Calhame had several lime kilns, a flax mill and villages called Calhame, Calhame Mountain and Mc Laughlin's town and contains two hundred and twenty nine acres.

CAVANAWEERY- CABHÁN NA MAIRE? – Round hill of maghar?

We have so far failed to get a proper meaning for Cavannaweery, so in its absence, we will go with the meaning as given by the Donegal place name books of 1835. Cavannaweery was the home of Connolly Gage Esq. who lived in Finn lodge. Gage was the landlord over the manor of Castlefinn which contained the majority of townlands in the Urney part of Donegal. Cavannaweery contains one hundred and twenty nine acres.

CLADY (CHURCH LAND) – AN CHLÓIDIGH – 'the strong flowing one' 'the loud one'

972 A.D. "Murchadh Ua Flaithbheartaigh (lord of Aileach) went upon a predatory excursion into Cinel-Conaill, and took a great prey; but being pursued and overtaken, Murchadh was wounded, and died thereof at Dun Cloitighe, after communion and penance." Dun Cloitighe means "the fort of Clady".

Clady takes its name after the river (the back burn) that flows into the river Finn. The Civil Survey of 1654 writing about Urney says it "hath nothing in it remarkable, and is bounded with the river Morne on the east & with a Brooke called Clady Brooke, on ye south"

Clady was one of the most historic places of our early history, been the first fording place on the Foyle system. For this Strategic reason, Clady and the surrounding area was the scene of many battles between the O Donnell's and the O Neill's and in the 1600's between the armies of King James and King William. Slater's directory (1870) for Clady mentions "in the neighbourhood are the ruins of O'Cahan's Castle". Early names in Clady (1666) are John Boyd, John Patrick, Mathew Patrick and John Allen. Clady contains one hundred and seventy three acres.

CLOGHFIN - AN CHLOCH FHIONN – the white stone.

Cloghfin contains two hundred and twenty eight acres. Samples of names that appear on Griffith's Valuation are Andrew Sproule, Elizabeth Griffin, John Kelly and William Devine. Villages, Broomfield and Cloghfin.

CORMAKILLY – CORA MHIC GIOLLA? – The weir of Mac Giolla?

The holy well of St Bridget is situated in a field in Cormakilly and down through the years has been a place of pilgrimage for many people. It contains one hundred and ninety two acres. Farms sold in Cormakilly (1917) were called Ned's land (40 acres 0 roods 15 perch) and Dudgions land (16 acres).

COOLYSLIN – CÚIL NA SLINNE – corner of the flat stone/ slate

On a map of the Manor of Castlefinn in 1816, Coolyslin takes up an area of about half its modern size on the upper side of the townland. The lower half next to the River Finn was called "Drumnaha". Richard Griffith who was head of the Valuation Department set up to value all townlands for rating purposes may have amalgamated these, leaving only one Drumnaha in the parish of Urney. Coolyslin now contains one hundred and fifty eight acres.

In the year 600A.D, a battle is believed to have taken place here between Cenel Conaill (O Donnell) and Cenel Eogain (O Neill), "battle of Cul Slemna" in which Cenel Eogain was the victor.
Villages – upper Coolyslin and lower Coolyslin

DONEYGOWEN – DÚN AN GHABHANN? – Fort of the Smith?

Doneygowen contains fifty four acres on the edge of Clady. Griffith valuation of 1857 States that Owen Lafferty had a lease on thirty two acres of land, house, offices, fishery, and the Flax-mill from Rev. Peter B. Maxwell.

DONEYLOOP/DUNNALOOB – DÚN NA LÚB – fort of the bends

The fort that Doneyloop takes its name from was located on top of the mound were the church of St. Columba's and its graveyard now stand. It contains thirty six acres and in 1816 was owned by Connolly Gage Esq.
Village - Doneyloop

DRESNAGH – DREASTARNACH – place of brambles

Dresnagh contains one hundred and twenty four acres belonging to Connolly Gage Esq. (1816). The names of people who paid Tithe's in 1827(tax used for the upkeep of the church of Ireland) were Bogan, Congland (Coneglan), and Dougherty.
Village – Dresnagh

DRUMBANE – AN DROIM BÁN – the white ridge.

"The aforesaid Quarter of Drumbane is known after the name of Ballamaclier and contains 11 and ½ Sessiaghs, known by several names fallowing, Drimbana,

Drumtigh-Connell, Druimna mallraeigh, drumtigh-mackye, drumnahil, skionbuy, gortcellagh, grapagh, drumnahath, ferean alias charagmore, carranambuihall and Tulliard=1/2 sessiagh.(taken from 1835 name books, Donegal)."

There was a holy well in Drumbane in 1816 and the townland contains ninety eight acres.

Villages - Drumbane, Flushtown.

DRUMNAHA –DROIM NA HÁTHA - ridge of the kiln

Drumnaha, a Sessiagh of Drumbane (drumnahath) Contains eighty two acres. Lafferty, Faulkner, and Bogan were names connected to the area in the early 1800's.

Villages – upper Drumnaha and lower Drumnaha.

DRUMDOIT – DROIM DÓITE - burnt ridge

In the early 1800's Drumdoit had a lime stone quarry, lime kiln, smiths forge and a flax mill. Names connected to the area at that time are Martin, Dogherty, Jack and Barron. Jacks lane is called after the Jack family with Robert Jack having a field at the end of the lane (1816). Drumdoit contains three hundred and ninety seven acres.

Village – Drumdoit.

FEARN – FEARNA - the alders

Fern, a Sessiagh of Drumbane (ferean alias charagmore) is the biggest townland in Urney at nine hundred and four acres, and at seven hundred and fifty five feet high is also the highest. Iron ore from Fearn hill was transported to London and used for the building of the old Wembley stadium. A battle is believed to have taken place in Fern (battle of Fornocht, 727A.D) in which Cenel nEogain defeated Cenel Conaill.

Villages - Fearn big and Fearn little, Tully and Magherabrack (speckled plain)

FORTTOWN (church land, 1654)

Forttown is called after the fort believed to have been built 2,500 thousand years. Since records began (1821), no one has ever lived in the townland of Forttown. Forttown contains thirty acres.

John Baird and Moses Sproule were tenant farmers here in 1858.

FOYFIN – NA FAICHÍ FIONNA – the white greens
Foyfin translates as 'the white greens' (Green lawn, garden).Foyfin has a total acreage of two hundred and thirteen acres and in 1836 contained only one house valued at over £5, that of Andrew Gamble.
Villages – Upper Foyfin, Lower Foyfin.

GLENTOWN (church land, 1654)
Glentown has a total area of two hundred and thirty acres, and names connected to the area in the 1860's are James Purdon, Thomas Henderson, Michael Scanlan and Joseph Love.
Village – Glentown.

GORTKILLY – GORT COILLE - Field of (the) wood, or wood-field
Gortkilly, a Sessiagh of Drumbane (gortcellagh), has a total of one hundred and forty three acres. Locals tell of an old graveyard from early times in Gortkilly. Tithes were paid in 1827 by Patrick Birney, Michael and Thomas Bogan, and Manus and Murtagh Lefarty (lafferty).

GORTNAGRACE – GORT NA GREISE – the field of the attack or aggression
There is no mention of a battle in Gortnagrace, but it may be connected to battles in Coolyslin or Fern. It is a large townland of four hundred and eighteen acres with names connected to the area in the 1800's been Rolleston, Brown, Maguire and a James Crawford who leased a house and forge from the Rev. Charles Irving.
Villages – Gortnagrace, Browne's town And Elliot's town.

GRAFFY –AN GHRAFAIDH - the grubbed land
Graffy, a Sessiagh of Drumbane (grapagh), contains one hundred and thirty six acres. It was from this townland that Honest John Kelly's father emigrated from in the early 1800's. Villages – Upper Graffy and Lower Graffy.

HALFTOWN – AN LEATHBHAILE
Halftown is shown as Drumconnel on Connolly Gage's maps of 1816, taking in Roganspark. Drumconnel is the Sessiagh mentioned in Drumbane, "Drumtigh-Connell". Halftown contains one hundred and six acres and H. McAnulty and Charles Holmes are mentioned in the 1816 maps. Villages - Halftown and Drumconnell.

HUNTERSTOWN – Eng. Hunter, a surname.

Hunterstown had a population of fifty one people in 1851, but by 1861 this had fallen to twelve with five families moving out presumably because of the effects of emigration and famine. Hunterstown takes in an area of thirty eight acres with the name Lafferty being predominant in Griffith's valuation.

INCHENNY - INIS EANAIGH (church land)
– island of the marsh (marsh-island)

957 A.D. "A plundering army was led to Inis Eanaigh by Fearghal O Ruaric; and the battle of Magh Itha was gained, wherein Aedh, son of Flaithbheartach, heir apparent of Cinel-Eoghain, was slain"

One of Urney's historic townlands where after the destruction of Grianan Aileach, Donnail MacLochlainn the last resident King of Aileach transferred his seat of power to Inchenny. Inchenny covers an area of one hundred and seventy three acres.

INCHENNY UPPER – INIS EANAIGH UACHTARACH
– island of the march (marsh island) Upper.

Inchenny Upper contains one hundred and sixty nine acres, and in 1841 had a population of 52. However by 1851 this had fallen to 27, with three families leaving the area.

INNISCLAN – IONASCLAINN – moorland

Innisclan takes in an area of three hundred and eighty four acres. In 1841 the population of Innisclan was 133, but had fallen to 84 by 1851, with ten families moving out of the area.

KELLY'S MEADOW – Eng. Kelly, a surname.

Kelly's Meadow is the smallest townland in Urney at three acres, one rood and nineteen perches and was at one time part of the townland of Millfarm.

KENNYSTOWN (church land) – Eng. Kenny, a surname.

Kennystown contains a total area of one hundred and two acres with names of m'loughlin, Colhoun and Scanlan leasing land from the Rev. William Knox in 1860.

LISDOO – AN LIOS DUBH – the black enclosure or ringfort.
Lisdoo with 166 people had one of the largest populations of any townland in Urney in 1841. However it was to suffer from the famine and emigration falling to 36 by 1891. Names in Lisdoo for the hearth money roll of 1666 were William Simpson, Robert faall? And Donold O'Boggan. The total area of Lisdoo is three hundred and thirty one acres.

MAGHERYCALLAGHAN – MACHAIRE ÚI CHEALLACHÁIN – plain of Ó Ceallacháin.
One hundred and forty four acres of some of the best land on the Donegal side of Urney. James M'Curdy leased all of Magherycallaghan from Connolly Gage Esq. In 1836; he had a scutch mill built which still stands today.

MILLFARM – FEIRM AN MHUILINN.
A townland also leased by M'Curdy who sublet five cottages to undertennants. These presumably were the workers for M'Curdy's mills and farm.
Millfarm contains twenty eight acres

MULLANBOY – AN MUILEANN BUI – the yellow mill.
In 1694 the mill at Mullanboy was let to Wm. Young and his wife Mary along with a Sessiagh of land called Mullanboy and half Sessiagh of Demaines. An agreement was made on the 1st September 1748? between Wm Connolly Esq. and John and Michael Stevenson of Coolyslin and Hugh Stevenson of Mullanboy binding them to use the mill at Mullanboy. Mullanboy covers a total area of sixty three acres.
Village – Mullanboy and Ring's End

RABSTOWN (church land) – Eng. Rab = Robert, personal name.
Samuel lewis topographical dictionary of Ireland (1836) states that Rabstown is glebe land let out to tenants. Rabstown covers an area of two hundred and six acres. In the Griffith valuation Rev. John M'conaghy had a lease of 18 acres from the landlord. On this land he had four cabins which he sublet to farm labours.

ROGAN'S PARK – Eng. – Rogan, O'Rouagain, surname.
Rogan's park, one of more recent new townlands in Donegal which at one stage was part of Drumconnell/Halftown (1816). It covers an area of nine acres.

SCOTSTOWN (church land) Eng. Scott, a surname.
The first mention of a man named Scott was a William Scott in Lower Urney in 1666. Names in the area were Purdon, Maxwell and Martin in 1860. It covers an area of eighty five acres.

SOMERVILLESTOWN (church land)
Home townland of one of Urney's oldest buildings, Urney Presbyterian Church. Somervillestown has an area of ninety three acres.

STEPHENSTOWN (church land) – Eng. Stephens, surname.
One hundred and twenty six acres of fertile land along the River Finn with a house valued at £7 in Griffith's valuations leased to Samuel Knox. A Thomas Stevinson (Stevenson) resided in Urney in 1622. (Derry diocese wills)

SKELPY – An Scealpaigh – the rocky cliff or chasm
The place name books of Donegal lists five lime kilns and three villages in Skelpy, upper, Middle and lower Skelpy. It contains two hundred and seventy eight acres.

SKERRYGLASS – An Sceirigh Ghlas? – the green rocky place
Also called Corryglass (1816). This would change its meaning to "the green weir". Skerryglass takes in an area of eighty seven acres with tenants by the names of m'Cawley, M'Daid, Dogherty and M'Cormack in Griffith's valuation.

TULLYARD –An tulaigh Ard - the high hillock
"Cut out old benty bog (reclaim!)" "Bog partly tilled (crop hopeless)" the quality of the some of the land in the early 1800's. Tullyard has an area of one hundred and thirty one acres Villages – upper and lower Tullyard.

TULLYMOAN – Tulaigh mhoáin – Hillock of Moán
Moán was the name of an ancestor of the Cineal Moáin, a branch of Cineal Eoghain, whose chieftain was O' Gairmleadhaigh or O' Gormlaigh (Gormley). Their territory was on the west of the Foyle until they were driven over to the Tyrone side by the O'Donnnells. The name suggests that it may have been an inaugural site of the chieftain.

URNEY – An Urnaí – A prayer/ The oratory

The town land of Urney covers an area of two hundred and eighteen acres with Richard Hamilton, John Gwynne, Hannah Flaherty and John Boyle holding land here in 1858.

URNEY GLEBE (church land) – Gléib na hUrnaí.

Also called "Cooledroman, glebe land". (Civil Survey 1664)."The Glebe of Urney called Cooledroman". (Tyrone down survey). Urney Glebe contains one hundred and fifteen acres of the best land in Urney and was held Freehold by the Rev. Benj. B. Gough in 1860.

MAPS OF THE MANOR OF CASTLEFINN

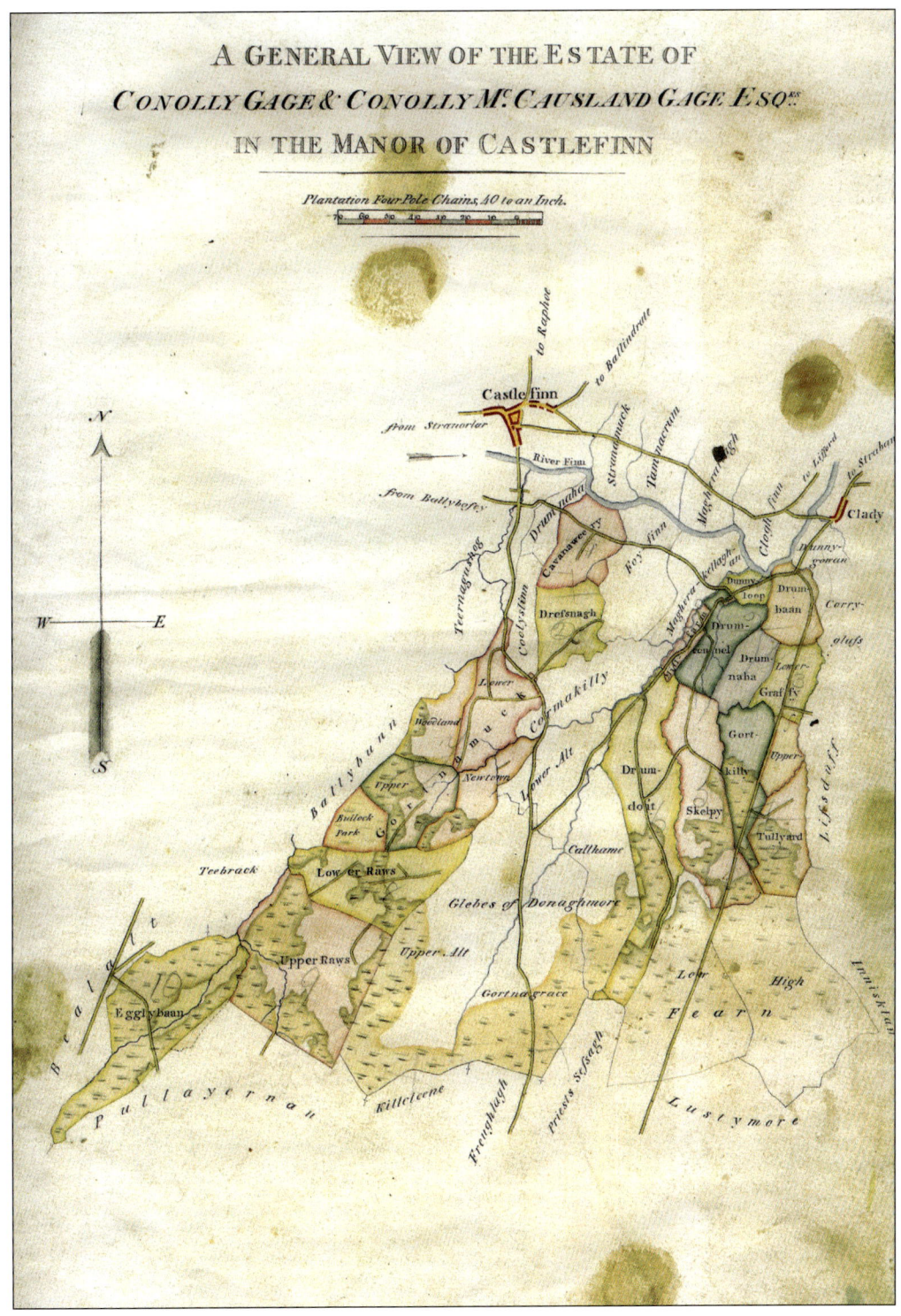

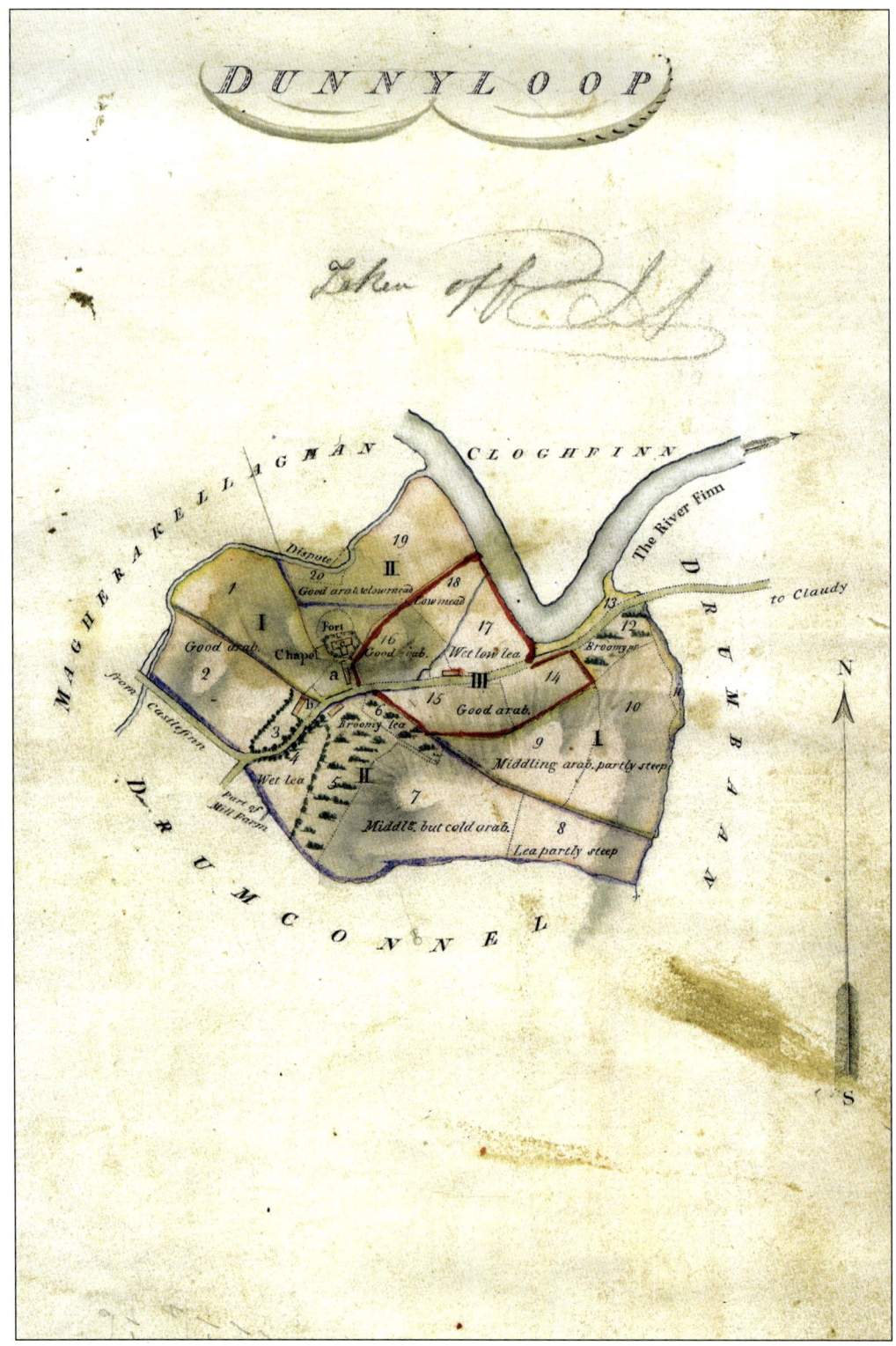

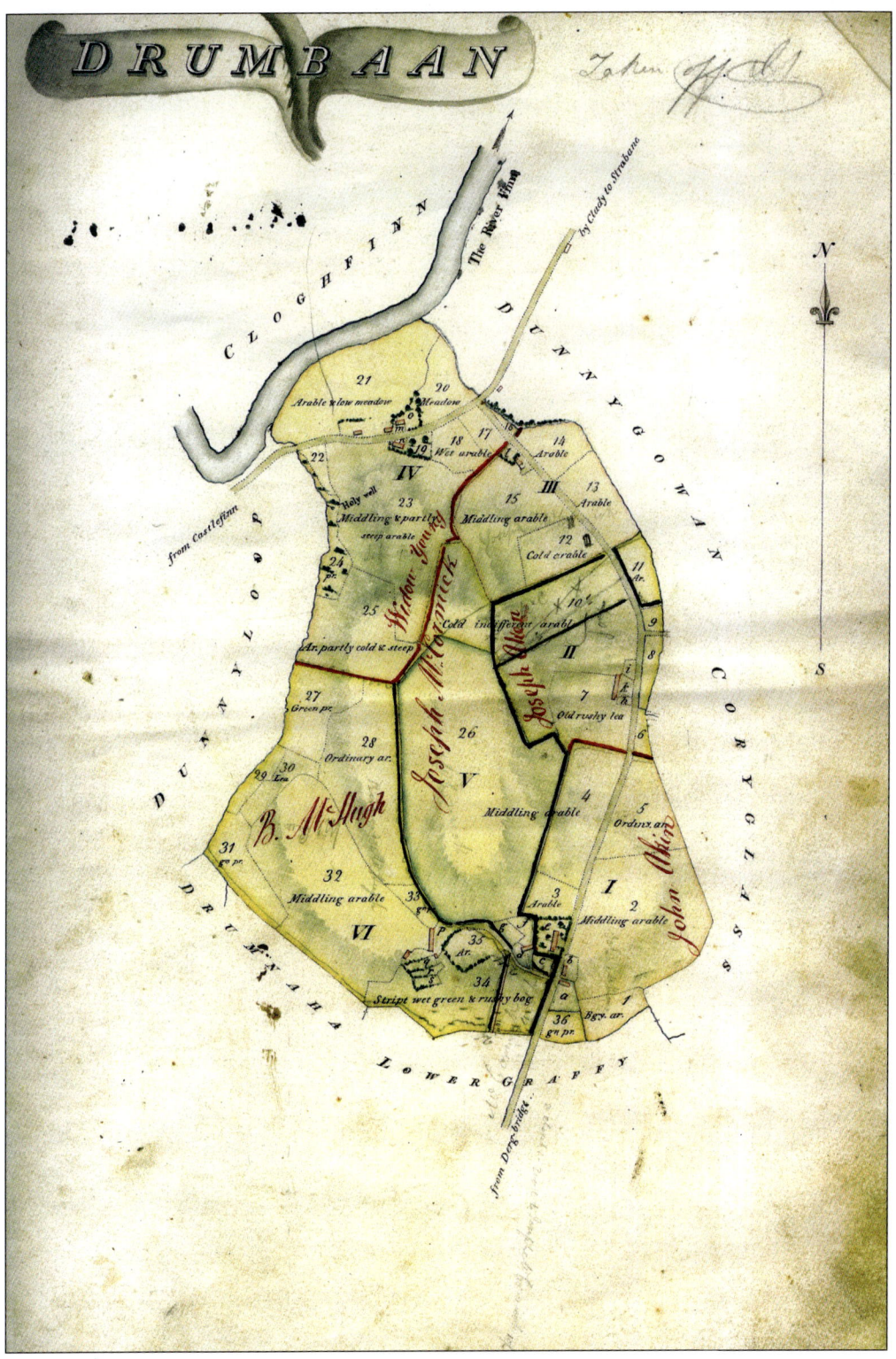

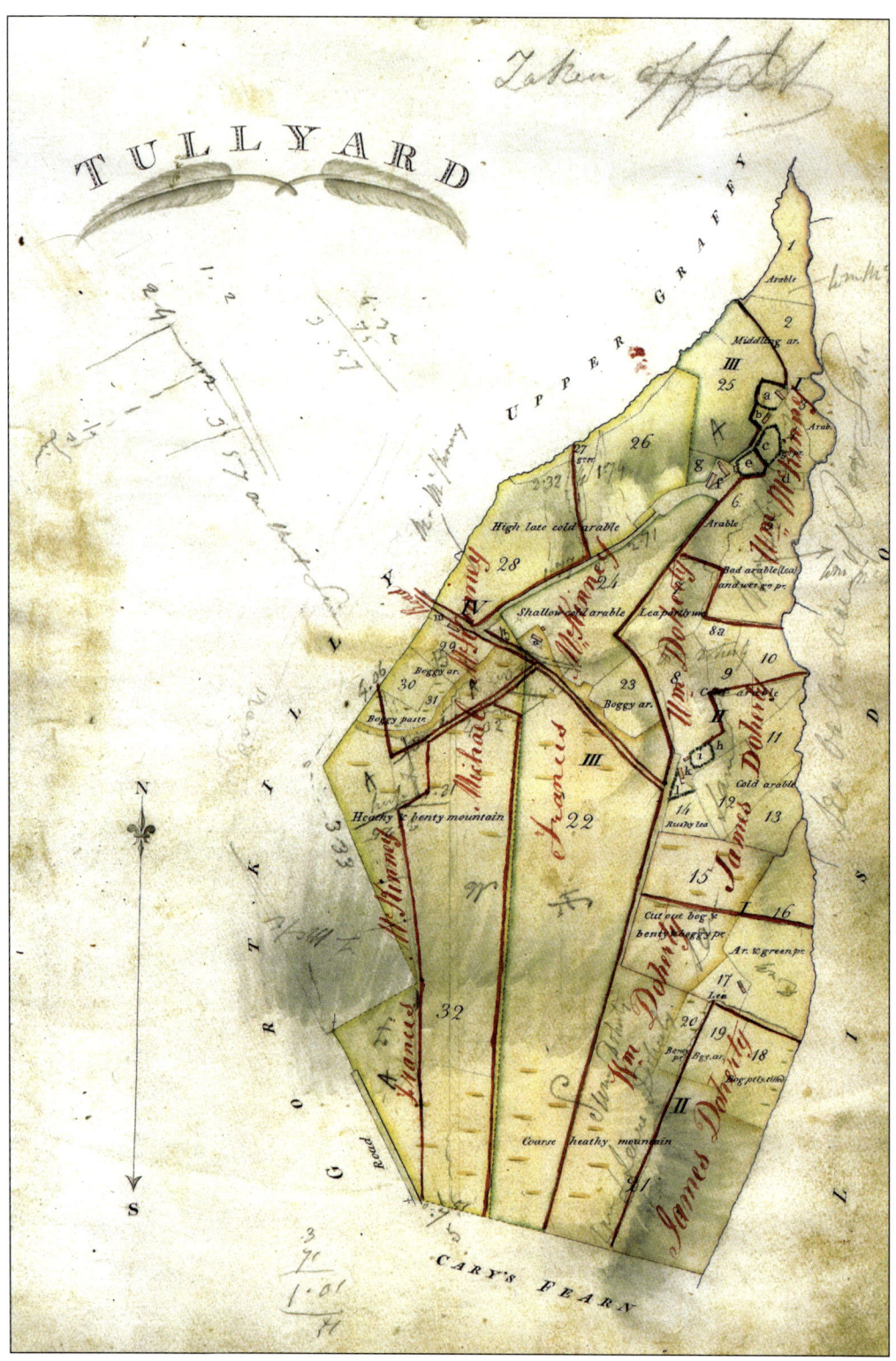

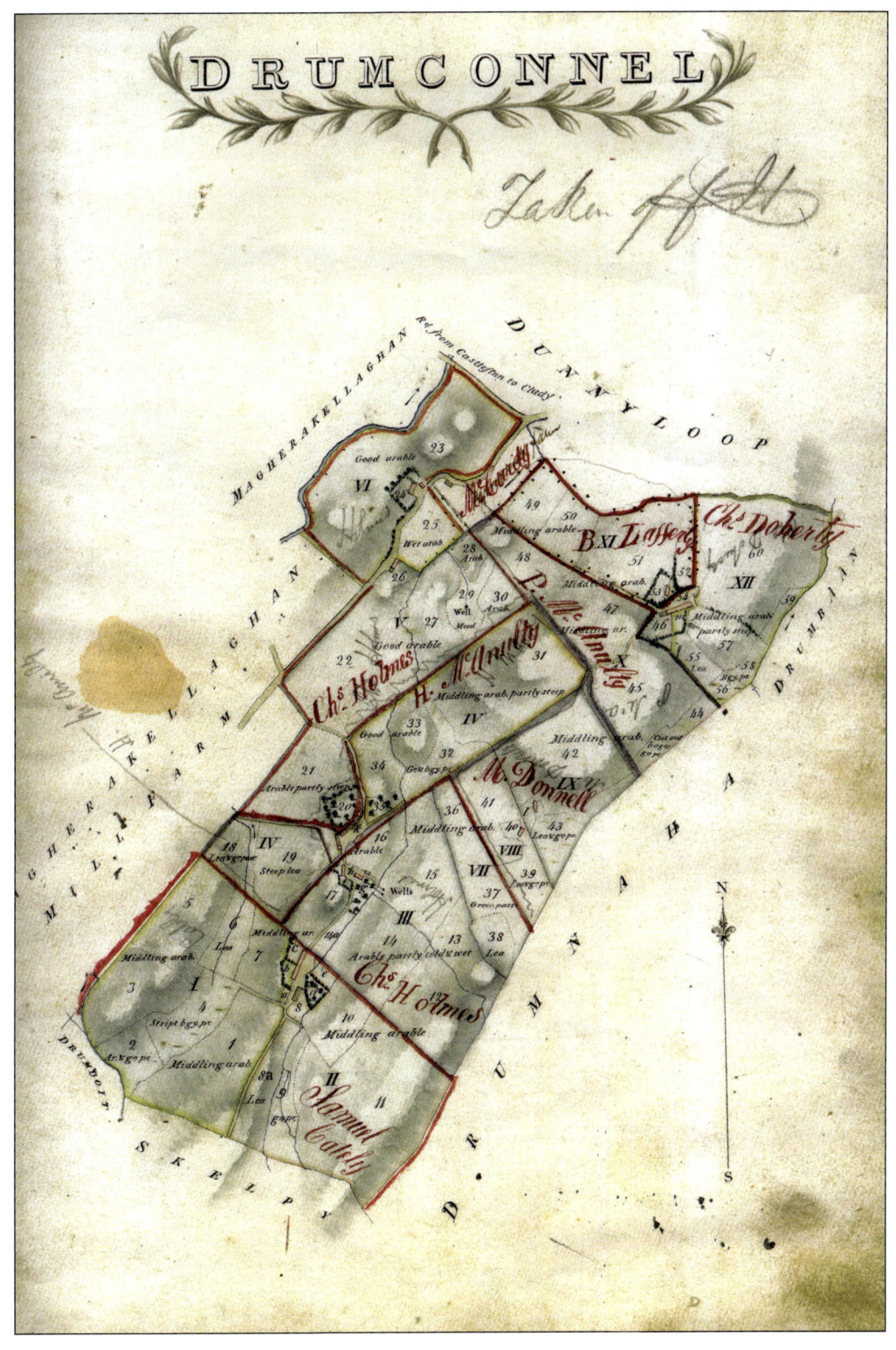

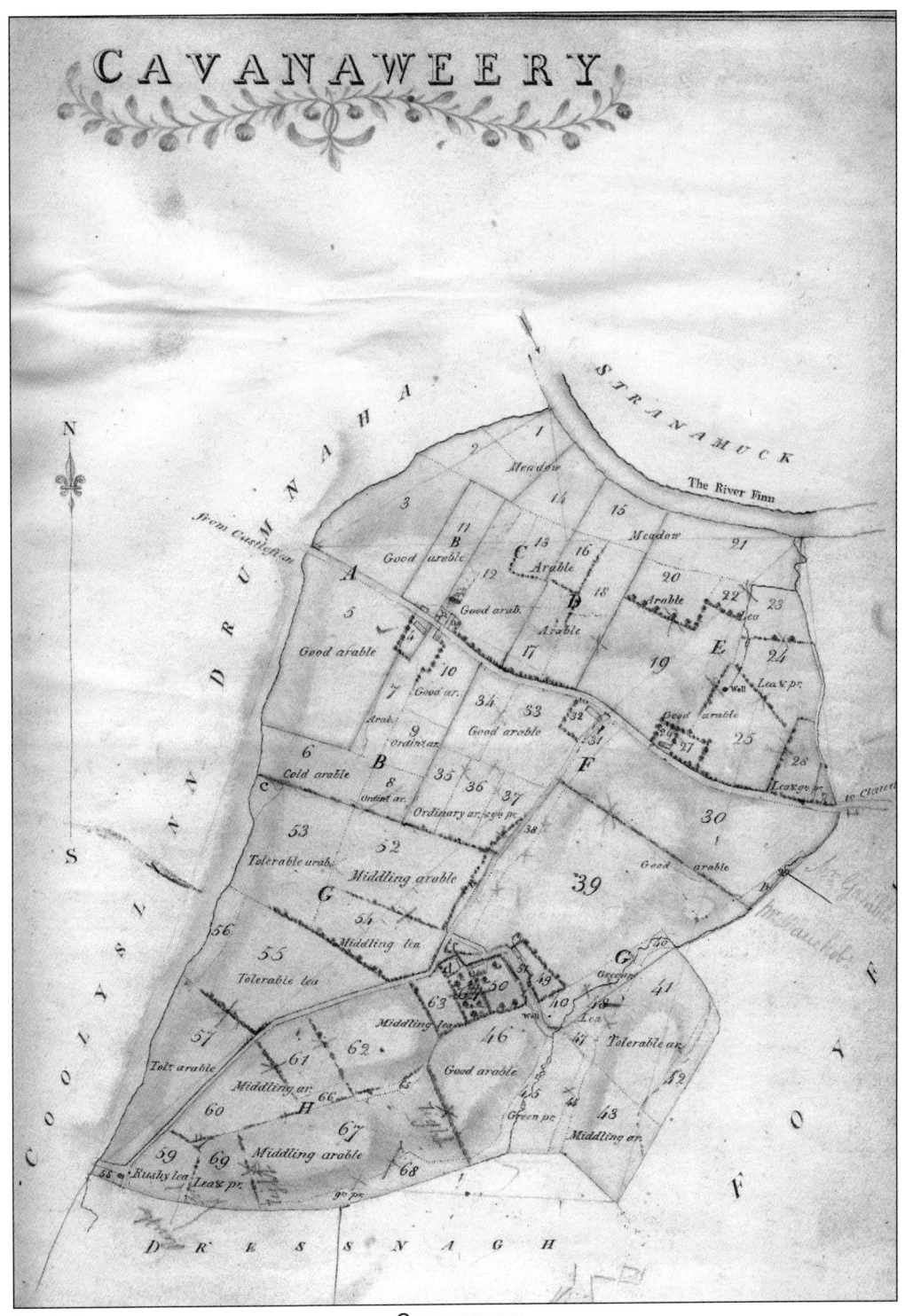

Cavanaweery

Lower Drumdoit

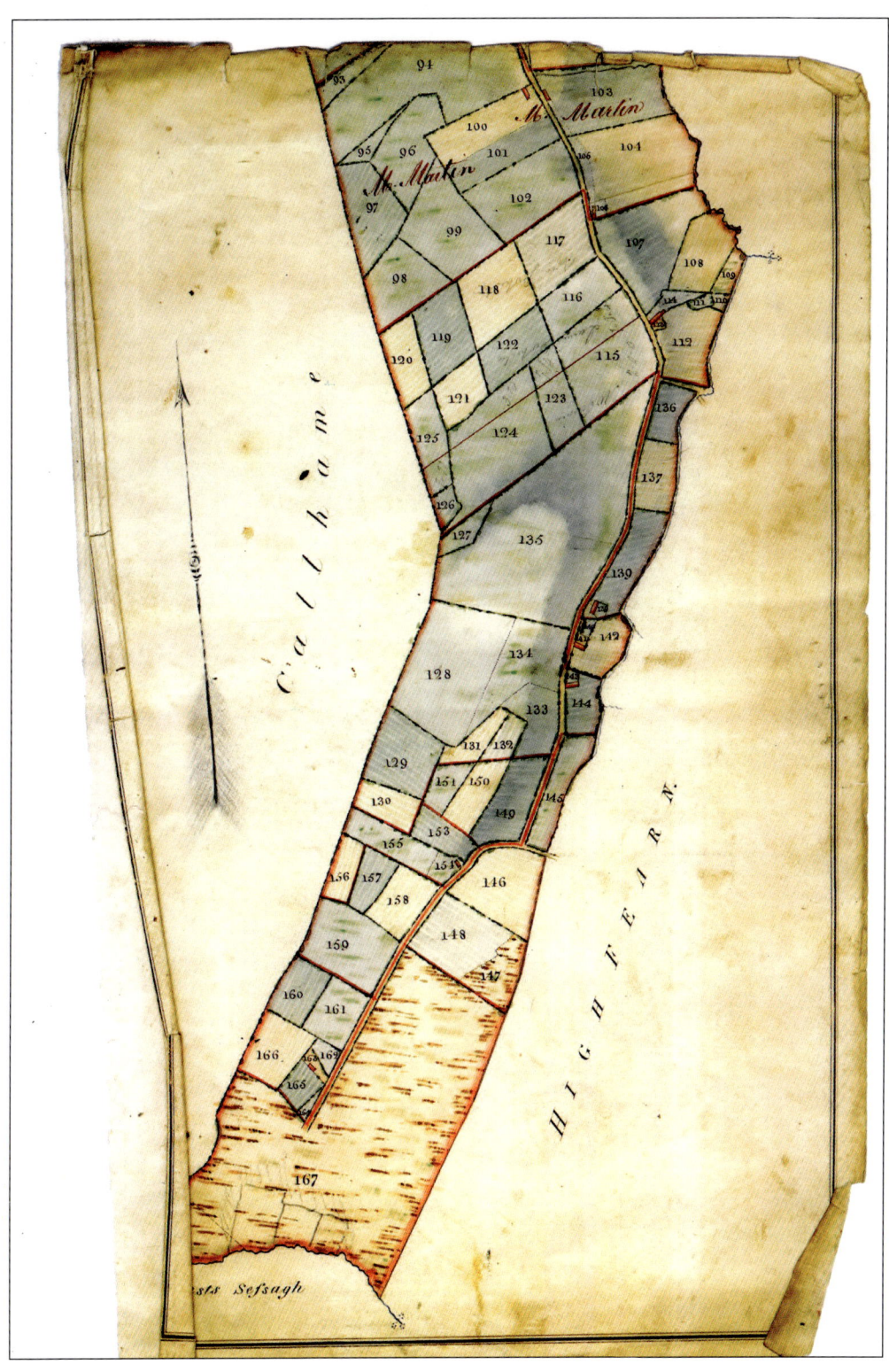

Upper Drumdoit

The Field

Townlands were not the only named areas of land in Ireland. Most if not all fields had names which have been passed on down through the years. A good few areas had a 'kill field'. You can be sure that a lime kiln was not far away. The 'kill field' at Alt Upper still has a lime kiln that has been used in living memory. Other fields in Alt include 'the back wood', 'McKane's field', Keenan's field' and 'the dam field'. 'The cairn' was the name on the field in which the Giants grave used to stand. Alt Lower has a 'moonlight hill' with the 'long dale' in Drumdoit.

The names of local farmers have stayed in the locality with 'Watsons land' and Falkners hill in Drumnaha. Other fields in Drumnaha were called 'the croft', 'the trench' and 'the goose hill'. 'The gillett field', also in Drumnaha has some interesting history. Both Michael Collins and Éamon De Valera are believed to have held rallies for the Clady Battalion of the I.R.A. at 'the gillett' which at that time was ideal for large clandestine gatherings.

A lot of field names had to do with the quality of the land, or a feature or building such as the lime kills mentioned. The 'water lea' field in Inchenny was a good dry field and the 'bog meadow' had dark heavy soil. The 'spout field' had indeed a water spout and the 'wee field' was small at 3 acres. Another field in Inchenny was given the name 'hall field' because it could be seen from the hall of the farm house.

Many more fields in Urney have very interesting names and stories attached which may be lost to history as farms change hands to the younger generation or as they are incorporated into single fields. With maps for farms now needed for government grants, it would not take long for individual land owners to mark down on a spare map the names of fields for future generations.

Early names in Urney

Year	Name	Year	Name
1621	Wm Hamilton (summonister roll)	1693	Thomas Parker (inquisition jury)
1621	Wm Craford (summonister roll)		Michael Semple (inquisition jury)
1630	Con O'Gormely (Inquisition Jury)	1694	James Spier (inquisition jury)
1625	Rich Babington (summonister roll)		Wm Younge and his wife Mary
1626	Jn Stensonon(Tyrone Quarter sessions)		(alias Phillips). Lease of mill, Mullanboy.
1628	John Bonham (wills of Derry Diocese)	1700	Robert Boyd (wills of Derry Diocese)
1630	John Bathurst (wills of Derry Diocese)	1720	James Fitzgerrald (wills of Derry Diocese)
1659	John Brown (wills of Derry Diocese)		
1660	John Spier (Urney parish poll tax book)	1722	John Fenton (wills of Derry Diocese)
	Donell M'Fadden (Urney poll tax book)	1748?	Michael Stevenson, John Stevenson, Coolyslin, Hugh Stevenson, Mullanboy, (lease of corn ground)
	Manus Finston(Urney poll tax book)		
1666	William Caldwell, Inchenny (H.M.R.)		
	Manus Finton, Lower Urney (H.M.R.)		
	John Speare, Inchenny (H.M.R.)	1750	Wm Hunter (wills of Derry Diocese)
	William Scott, Lower Urney (H.M.R.)	1752	Hodgson Gage, (Purchase of Manor of Castlefinn.)
	Donold O'Boggan, Lisdoo (H.M.R.)		
1680	Caal O'Dogherty, Inisclan (H.M.R.)	1753	Wm Maxwell (wills of Derry Diocese)
1686	John Boyd, Clady. (Urney poll tax book)	1760	Robert McGhee (wills of Derry Diocese)
	John Crawford(Urney poll tax book)	1776	Robert Sproule (wills of Derry Diocese)
	Robert Haire (Gortakilly,Churchwarden)		James Knox (wills of Derry Diocese)
1692	Wm Hamilton (Churchwarden)	1780	Mary, Nail and John O'Bogan, Dunnaloob, (lease of Dunnaloob.)
	John Browne (inquisition jury)		
	John Hamilton (inquisition jury)	1788	Saml Brown, Maghercallaghan (to quit claim to Mill at Maghercallaghan.)
		1799	Daniel McGinley (wills of Derry Diocese)
			Henery O'Neill, Claudy, (lease of part townland of dresnagh.)

H.M.R. – Hearth Money Roll

The Great Hunger
By Daniel Mc Menamin

Ireland as a country lacked the mineral resources that led other countries into the industrial revolution of the eighteenth and nineteenth century. What we did possess in great quantity and quality was land, rich pasture that although not owned by the farmer class was able by subsistence farming to feed the majority of the rural people of Ireland. In the early 1800's, there was an increasing shift to tillage farming needing increased labour and with the Irish making the potato their main source of food, allowed the population grow substantially over a short period of time. The population of Ireland in 1800 stood at five million. This increased to over eight and a half million by the time of the great famine. The potato blight first struck in the autumn of 1845 with a partial failure of the potato crop but by 1846 there was a total failure. The poorer people were almost totally dependent on the humble potato; a working man could eat 14lbs of potatoes in one day. It was their breakfast and dinner, and this dependence now led to their death from starvation and diseases such as typhus and dysentery.

The people of Urney were not immune from the great famine. There was an estimated 1,533 people destitute in Urney in the years 1846/47, this out of a population of around 7,500 people. It was not the first time Urney had suffered such distress. The famine of 1741 known by the Irish as bliain an áir 'year of slaughter' caused by a great frost followed by a prolonged drought killed around 400,000 thousand people out of a population of 2.4 million. A famine in 1744/46 was most severe in the north west of Ireland caused by a deficient harvest coupled with livestock disease and in 1783; a meeting took place in Urney Church about a famine which had started the year before. Many people looked for help in the workhouse in Strabane, a system of relief set up by the poor law of 1838 to take care of the very poor. This was a last resort for the poor people of the Urney area. Families were separated on entry and were not allowed contact with each other. They were given just enough rations to keep them alive but even though there was a resident doctor, forty five people died during one week in 1847. Many people on knowing their fate entered the workhouse to ensure a decent burial.

Thomas Gilroy left his native Manorhamilton in August 1847 with his wife and six children in search of work in Glasgow. There was little work to be got and following a fever which killed two of his children he was given money for the boat to Derry. They were turned away from the workhouse in the city as they had no transfer documentation and advised to go to Strabane. The family arrived at Strabane workhouse hungry, weak and exhausted having only eaten raw turnips. They were again sent away for having no official identification. An old women gave them shelter in her cabin in Melmount were they lay on the floor. The next morning Thomas Gilroy and his youngest child died. The rest of the family were let into the workhouse.

Many more people died in the wretched cabins where they lived, in the streets of towns and villages, and by the sides of roads where they huddled up to their loved ones awaiting their doom. The clergy of the area asked their parishioners to take the names of people destitute on the roads in order for them to be identified when they died.

The policy of the establishment in England did not help the destitute, "Irish property must pay for Irish poverty" "Irishmen could live on anything . . . there was plenty of grass in the fields even though the potato crop should fail". Despite government indifference about the Great Famine, many organisations and individuals tried to help the Irish people. The Marquis of Abercorn as well as having a soup kitchen employed up to 600 men on his estate, The Society of Friends (quakers) although only 200 in number in Ireland provided help away and above what would be expected of them and the Choctaw Indian tribe of Oklahoma, on hearing of the famine sent $170 in Famine relief funds.

The potato crop remained below the 1844 level until 1854. By 1851, one million people had died in the great famine and a further one million people had emigrated to America and Canada, with a great number (up to 40%) dying on the 'coffin ships' and at Grosse Isle, a quarantine island on the St. Lawrence River. Grosse Isle today bears a monument to 5,424 people who "found in America but a grave".

The World at War

By Daniel Menamin

On the 8th June 1914 in the town of Sarajevo a Bosnian Serb by the name of Gavrilo Princip shot and killed the heir to the Austro-Hungarian Empire Archduke Franz Ferdinand starting a war that would claim the lives of over 9,000,000 soldiers and 5,000,000 civilians. Up to 300,000 Irish soldiers fought in the Great War as it was called with an estimated 35,000 men from all over the island killed.

Irishmen joined the war effort for many reasons. Some joined up for adventure in foreign lands, others joined to put food on the table, what James Connolly called "economic conscription". Others fought and died for King and Country and others still fought and died for a free Ireland. The Home Rule Bill that was passed in 1912 and due to come into effect in 1914 was, on the outbreak of World War One suspended until after the war. The Ulster Volunteer Force founded in 1913 to protect Ulster against Home Rule was now called on by Edward Carson "to answer immediately his Majesty's call". John Redmond called on the Irish Volunteers to support the war effort, believing not unreasonably that the sooner the war was over, the sooner the Home Rule Bill could be implemented. In a speech made in the House of Commons he said "the armed Nationalist Catholics in the south will only be too glad to join arms with the armed Protestant Ulstermen ". This was to split the Irish Volunteers with a large majority following Redmond to form the National Volunteers.

Thousands of men from all over Ireland joined the new army Divisions, the 10th (Irish) Division, the 16th (Irish) Division and the 36th (Ulster) Division as well as many other Regiments. The 10th Division fought among other places at Gallipoli and Palestine. The 16th Division fought in the Bethune taking part in the battle of Messines along with the 36th Division. The 36th Division also fought on the first day of the battle of the Somme losing 2069 men.

Back in Ireland a rising took place on Easter Monday 1916 in which members of the Irish Republican Brotherhood (IRB) and the Irish Citizen Army led by Patrick Pearce took over the centre of Dublin. After several days fighting, Dublin was again under the control of the government and the people of Dublin were angry at the Rising leaders for the destruction of Central Dublin. This however changed when military courts executed 16 of the Rising leaders turning the people against the Government. Tom Kettle, a former nationalist MP for East Tyrone said of the 1916 leaders, they "will go down in history as heroes and martyrs; and I will go down- if I go down at all-as a bloody British Officer". Kettle was killed at the Somme on the 9th September 1916.

World War one ended when the Armistice was signed at 6a.m on the 11th November 1918. Soldiers returned to an Ireland much changed from when they had left. Ulster Protestants returned triumphant, heroes from battles like the Somme, Messines and Ypres knowing what they fought for and knowing what they wanted. Irish Nationalist on the other hand returned home not knowing what they had fought for. The Easter Rising had given nationalist Ireland its martyrs leaving soldiers who had fought for a free Ireland on the bloody battle fields of World War One disillusioned, without the jubilant homecoming crowds of a grateful Nation and in time an Irish Government unwilling to acknowledge the islands war dead.

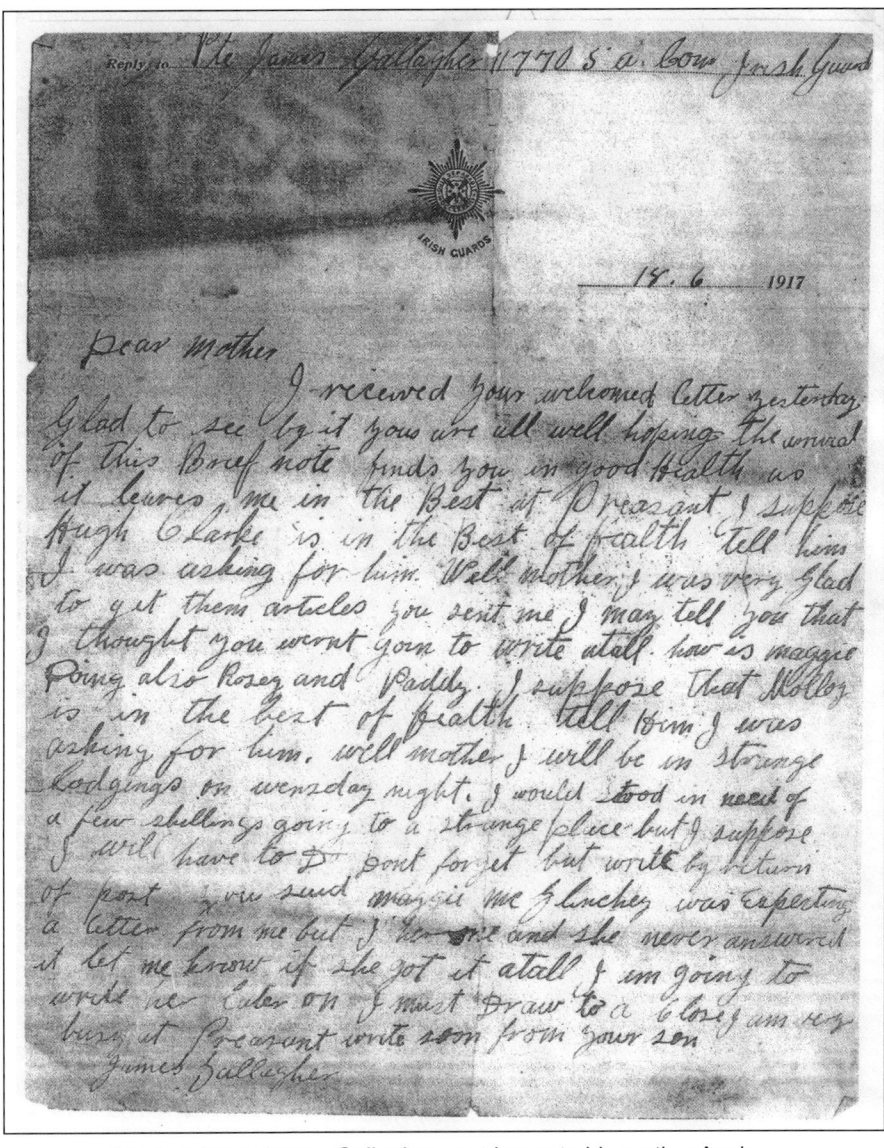

The last letter James Gallagher sent home to his mother Annie

Urney's World War One Dead

Robert Bogle, Mullanbouy.
Patrick Gallagher, Alt Lower.
Samuel Gilchrist, Alt.
John Kerrigan, Mullanbouy.
Joseph Roulston Mortland, Ringsend.
Patrick Mc Philomey, Urney West, (Donegal).
Patrick Cullen, Doneyloop, Urney.
James Worling
Hugh Mountgomery Archdale Olphert
John James Worling
William Moorhead
Mathew Nelson
Hugh Mc Kelvey
Jack Mc Kelvey
George Mc Cutcheon
Samuel Hamilton
Robert Darragh
George Bustard
John Anderson
William John Gormley, Flushtown.
John Frederic Kennedy
George Foster
John James Gordon
Samuel Hall
David Reid
George H. Wiseheart
James Love, Glentown.
James Park, Innisclan.
Oliver Stevenson, Magheragar.
James Gallagher, Clady.

The British War and Victory medals of James Gallagher, Clady.

> I hereby acknowledge the receipt of the British War and Victory medals granted in respect of the service of the late N°11770 Guardsman J. Gallagher Irish Guards.
>
> Date Sep. 9th 1922.   Signature Annie Gallagher

A Nation Divided

By Daniel Mc Menamin

The GAA was formed in 1884 to promote Gaelic sport and culture and was part of a larger trend towards a cultural and nationalist revival at the time. Various groups were formed around this time, Conradh na Gaeilge was founded in 1893, Cumann na nGaedheal in 1900 and the The Sinn Fein party in 1905 to name a few.

One Urney resident who took an active part in this revival was Denis Phelan. Denis was born in Stephenstown outside Clady in 1880. His parents were Denis and Matilda (nee Mc Cutcheon). He was appointed as a postman in 1898 and was transferred to Glenties in 1902. Denis was a lifelong Republican joining the Wolfe Tone Association in 1900 and Sinn Fein in 1906. As a supporter of the I.R.A., his home in Glenties was raided several times by the Royal Irish Constabulary (R.I.C.) and the Black and Tans. He took the Republican side during the civil war and was a founder member of Fianna Fail setting up the Charlie Daly Cumann in Glenties. He served as a County Councillor 1925/26 and stayed loyal to the party until his death in August 1976.

Sam O' Flaherty from Castlefinn was another name within Republican circles in the war of Independence. He was elected to the 2nd Dáil as a T.D. at the 1921 election for Donegal. He was re-elected unopposed as an anti-Treaty Sinn Fein T.D at the 1922 election but did not take his seat. Sam originally from Clady led an arms raiding party against Drumquin R.I.C. barracks in December 1919 in which an R.I.C. man was killed. Another man on the raiding party was John James Kelly. John James was born in the Raws, Castlefinn in 1890. He was a man of the left who followed the socialist philosophy of James Connolly and often spoke to his son about Lenin. He joined the I.R.B. at a young age and formed a group of volunteers in Clady. He took part in many operations during the war of Independence and was arrested and imprisoned in England. After the foundation of the Irish Free State Kelly fought on against the newly formed Northern State. He died in 1938 when a bomb went off prematurely at Stranamuck outside Castlefinn.

> Your life one long attempt to free
> Your land and class from slavery.
> Unconquered Gael, your race is run,
> Your watch upon the hill is done.
> The Drumboe martyrs rush to greet
> The Connolly of Clady Street

Clady was the scene of many attacks during the early 1920's. On the 10th February 1922, up to 100 I.R.A. Volunteers attacked an Ulster Special Constabulary (B-specials) patrol in Clady. Charles Mc Fadden, one of the 'B- specials' was killed in the attack. A few days beforehand, two Unionist were kidnapped from the area by the I.R.A. This was in retaliation for the arrest of some members of the I.R.A. who were part of the Monaghan football team travelling to Derry. Several serious engagements between I.R.A. Divisions and Crown Forces took place in the Clady area after the signing of the Anglo Irish treaty in 1922. To stop attacks across the newly formed border, the Northern Government had the Clady Bridge blown up but this was repaired by the people of Clady.

A view of Clady Bridge

The boundary commission still held out hope for both Unionists and Nationalists that 'their area' would be included in their chosen state. Nationalists held out hope that the Boundary Commission would place the Clady area in the Free State. Unionists in Donegal demanded through the unionist delegation for Urney West to be included in Northern Ireland. After leaked notes of the negotiations, including a draft map that suggested that parts of east Donegal would be transferred to Northern Ireland, which would have been an embarrassment to the Free State Government, an agreement was reached keeping the original boundary of 1922.

> As they entered Clady
> Mc Fadden bold did stare
> When the strong voice of a Rebel shouted
> 'Halt and who goes there
>
> Then bang bang the rifles rang
> The specials turned and fled
> While Mc Fadden bold lay cold and dead
> With a bullet through his head

A glimpse at the parish of Urney

By John Rogan

NAME: The original Gaelic word *urnaí* indicates an activity rather than the name of a place. It means 'praying', and reminds us that the parish takes it name from the convent founded by St Cognat and from the primary activity that was carried on there. As far as can be ascertained, Urnaí and Camas at the Bann near Coleraine are the only two very early convents in the diocese of Derry. Indeed the Life of St Eoghan (Eugene) of Ardstraw speaks of him visiting, with St Tiarnach of Clones, a convent called *Ros Cay in terra Metheorun (*in the land of the ? Methei ?) Whose abbess was called *Mosseta*. Since the ancient name of the Lagan was Má Íotha, and in later times the parish was known as Uraní Mhá Íotha, it is not impossible that Urnaí was the place in question - in *terra Maighe Íotha*- with its name garbled by a later scribe unfamiliar with the area. Local knowledge may decide if Ros Cay can be identified. The only suggested date for the death of St Eoghan (Eugene) is the year 550. The account of his life is late and not particularly reliable.

CONVENT; Unfortunately, we have no historical record of anyone with a name like *Mosseta* in the convent of Urnaí. Apart from St Cognat, the founder, we know the names of some others, all venerated as saints in medieval times, who made the name of Urnaí famous: Feme, now Féimhe, pronounce fay've, (feast day 21.01), Fainche, pronounce *fan'***che**: -ch-as in *loch* (feast 01.01), Neas (feast 04.09), Sáfann (sámhthann) (feast 18.12). Safann later became abbess of Cluain Brónaigh (Clonbroney) near Granard, now in Co. Longford, was well known as a spiritual director and died in 739. The convent is unlikely to have survived the Viking era.

PARISH: Urnaí returns to the light of history in the twelfth and thirteenth centuries when parishes as we know them were being created. The development of Urney and Donaghmore shows most clearly one basis for division. Donaghmore was the *tuath* (state/kingship) of Clann Diarmada/ Ó Caireálláin (Carlin/ kerlin) whereas Urnaí was the *tuath* of Cineál Moain/ Ó Gormlaigh (O Gormley), two ruling septs who were continually at war, until Ó Gormlaigh proved victorious and forced Ó Caireálláin to move closer to their ally and over king, Mac Lochlainn, at Derry, where they gave their sept name, Clann Diarmada, to the parish of Clandermot/Glendermott. Ó Gormlaigh were allied to their over king Ó Néil, who was to prove the stronger. Ó Gormlaigh's territory included the present parishes of Urnaí, Mourne, Sion Mills and Camus. Later Ó Dónaill forced them across the river Mourne, and later still they were displaced towards Gortin by Ó Néill where they left the name of their branch of their sept in Munterloney/ Muintir Luinigh. The centralilty of Urnaí is underlined by the fact that the denery that includes the parishes in East Donegal and West Tyrone in the diocese of Derry was known in medieval times as the deanery of Má Íotha.

ERENAGH: Since the seventeenth century the parish church and clergy in Ireland are maintained by the direct offerings of the people of the parish. This was not always the case. From the thirteenth to the end of the sixteenth century land was set aside in each parish for this purpose. The land was farmed by the *aircheannach/ erenagh*. He was appointed by the bishop and his office continued in his family. He had also an obligation to provide for travellers and was involved in the education of the clergy in those days before seminaries, when to prepare for priesthood meant being apprenticed to a serving priest in a parish. In Urnaí, the erenagh was Ó Ceallaigh/ Ó'Kelly, of the branch known as Mac an Bhaird (Ó Ceallaigh). Obviously the name also shows that they were involved in literary matters. The bard was a grade of poet lower than the file, whose job was to declaim the poetry composed by the file. Being closely involved in parish life, the erenagh families produced most of the priests of the diocese in the Middle Ages, in this case including later, probably Tarlach Ó Ceallaigh/ Terence O' Kelly, vicar apostolic of Derry for some thirty years (1630-66) of that period of 119 years when the diocese had no bishop.

The Inquisitions held in 1610 to prepare for the Plantation reported on erenagh lands of each parish and the rents and tithes they paid to the bishop. Unfortunately they give no return for Urnaí. The 'good and lawful men' on the jury claimed they did not know what the rents were. Most of its members, except Ruairí Ó Gormlaigh, were from East Tyrone. Since coinage was scarcely in use at the time, many rents were paid in kind. Thus we know that, at Donaghmore, Ó Galáin, the erenagh, had to pay the bishop, amongst other things, '4 score meathers of malt' and Ó Cearbhalláin/ O'Carolan at Lifford paid '20 meathers of malt' a year. A meather/ *meadar* was a wooden vessel containing two gallons. The malt was for the bishop's beer, essential to the diet of the time, and is testimony to the fertility of Má Íotha.

CHURCHLANDS: In the erenagh system townlands in each parish were set aside for the upkeep of the parish, usually four, sometimes more. In the English grant to Established Church bishop George Montgomery in 1610 the erenagh lands are:

Aghenedonagh, Cogan, Nurim and Longford.

In 1615 Established Church bishop John Tanner was in receipt of:

Aghnedawnagh, Cogan Nurim and Longford.

In addittition there were two ballyboes (baile bó)/ townlands at Ballinlinny, a chapel of ease of Urnaí, from which the erenagh paid the bishop a yearly rent of two shillings and sixpence.

As listed in 1634 the church lands of Urnaí are:

Aghenedowagh, Cogan Nurim and Longford;

along with half a quater (= 2 ballyboes) at Ballynalinney

and 2 sessioghs of Ballylast near Lifford in the barony of Raphoe.

The spelling of these names was of course at the mercy of scribes unfamiliar with the area and probably not all that concerned with rendering the original Irish with accuracy. It can make for confusion and difficulty in sorting out what the names might mean. The name Longford would point to a settlement of Vikings/Norse in the area. The Civil Survey (1654) adds Cooledroman, glebe land, and gathers all the rest under the name 'Urney', leased to Matthew Babington, described as "English Protestant", although the rest of the parish had been granted to James Lord Hamilton, Baron Strabane, described as "Scottish Papist". Ballilast was leased to the heirs of James Spotswood. The district was planted from Scotland. During his tenure as vicar apostolic, appointed by the pope to run the diocese since there was no bishop, Terence O' Kelly probably lived under the protection of the Hamiltons at Urney.

ST BRIDGET'S WELL IN CORMAKILLY

In Penal days, a priest named Fr James Gallagher was saying Mass convenient to the well. The priest hunters were spotted by the lookouts on duty who warned the priest he had to flee. And old woman cried out, "don't go until you leave us some Holy water" and she handed him her tin can full of water. He blessed the water and flung the tin into the well. Then he blessed the well and said "All of you will get Holy Water from this well when I will not be here". Many people visit this well to this day.

THE STORY OF FR WARD

In times of persecution a priest named Fr Ward, who had had been hunted from Inis Eanaig came to Urney, he lived in a hut in the corner of a field in Glentown and said Mass in a disused gravel pit. On the night of a full moon, Priest hunters, two brothers named Fullerton came, he made out and they pursued him to the top of Fern Hill where they killed him. People discovered his body, where it lay convenient to the Mass centre of Drumdoit? They carried his body on a litter with hand spokes and buried him in an area known as the 'White Bog'. They put the willow hand spokes in the ground where they grew into trees a body's breadth apart. This spot is well known.

THE SEMINARIES

Fr Philip McDevitt was studying in Paris when he was appointed Bishop of Derry in 1766. He came back first to Moville but felt unwelcome by the civil authorities. He then came to Clady where he founded a little Seminary in a thatched house later known as the grove. He became president and professor. One of his student's notice tears of joy as he gave his first lecture to his students about a dozen in number. The catholic faith was rising again after many years of turmoil. About 1780 Bishop McDevitt moved to Derry, the first bishop to reside there for 180 years since the death of Bishop Redmond O'Gallagher in 1601, signs that the anti-catholic pressure has eased.

QUOTES FROM WILKINSON

A report by Lieutenant Wilkinson in March 1836 states that the people of Urney have a longer life span than many neighbouring parishes; many live into their 70s and 80s. This report also mentions that the size of Urney was 14357 acres. The 1st Church in Doneyloop was thatched and opened in 1735 by Fr Nugent and the 2nd was opened in 1824 by Fr Neil J O'Domnaill at a cost of £370

The patron Saint or our parish is St Feme although the church is dedicated to St Columba. Our church is situated in the townland of Doneyloop or in Irish Dún na lúb which is a reference to the bend in the river Finn which flows gently past a few yards away. It is about half a mile into Donegal from the Tyrone border, it is on a elevated site and in the gothic style. The architect was O'Neill from Belfast and cost £2000. It is 100ft long and 60ft wide and seats approx 440 people.

The opening sermon was preached by Fr William Ronan S.J. at a high mass at 11 O'clock, 18th October 1868. The collection amounted to £400. The spire, 100ft, and parochial house were built at a later date.

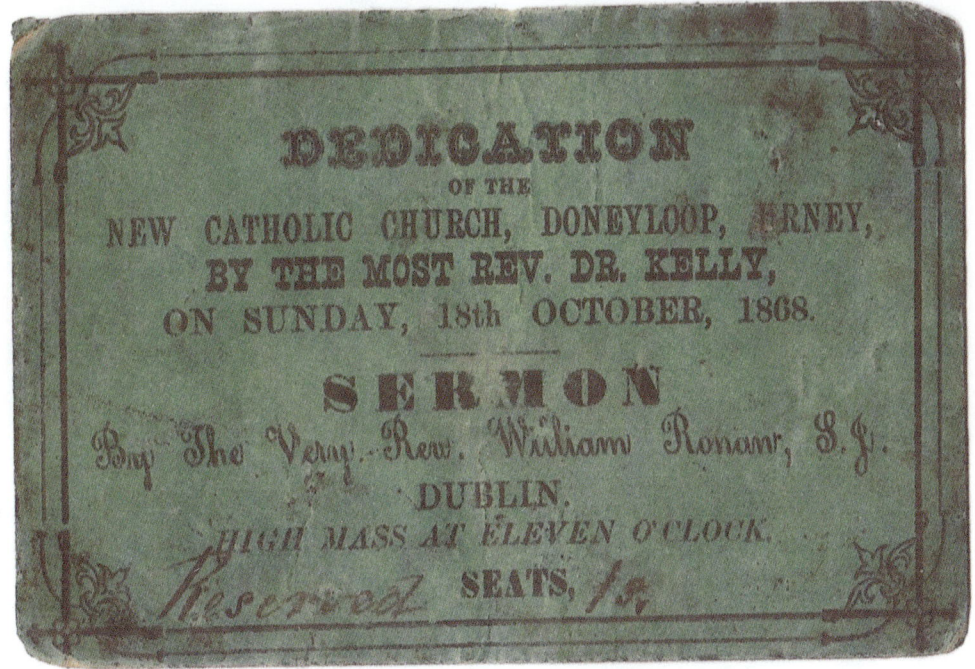

Above: Entrance ticket from the opening Sermon, which cost 1 shilling.

We associate the church with the most important moments of our lives: baptisms, confirmations, weddings, funerals, and the regular rhythm of Sunday worship, a tangible sign of a faith that has been handed onto us.

On entering the church you will see that it is a cruciform design and when you stand and look at the sanctuary area with its semicircular wall facing north. You will see there are six stained glass windows depicting St Eugene, St Peter, St Patrick, St Bridget, St Columcille, and St Paul.

SAINT EUGENE

Saint Eugene was an Irish monk who became the first bishop of Ardstraw, Tyrone, now the diocese of Derry. He was born in Leinster, and was a relative of St Kevin of Glendalough. Kidnapped as a child, he spent years as a slave before returning to Ireland. There he helped St Tigernach found Clones Monastery in 576.

SAINT PETER

The first pope, Prince of the Apostles, and founder, with St Paul, of the see of Rome. Peter was a native of Bethsaida, and worked, like his brother St Andrew, as a fisherman. Andrew introduced Peter to Jesus, and Christ called Peter to become a disciple. The first appearance of the Risen Christ was before Peter, ahead of the other disciples, and when the Lord came before the disciples at Tiberias, he gave to Peter the famous command to "Feed my lambs... Tend my sheep... Feed my sheep". Peter was crucified on the Vatican Hill upside down because he declared himself unworthy to die in the same manner as the Lord.

St Eugene and St Peter

SAINT PATRICK

Apostle of Ireland, born in Roman Britain c,387; As a boy of fourteen or so, he was captured during a raiding party and taken to Ireland as a slave to herd and tend sheep, Patrick's captivity lasted until he was twenty. He was ordained a bishop, and was sent to take the Gospel to Ireland. Patrick preached and converted many in Ireland for 40 years. After years of living in poverty, travelling and enduring much suffering he died on March 17, 461 at Saul, Downpatrick, Ireland where he had built the first church.

SAINT BRIDGET

St Brigid is one of Ireland's patron saints along with Saints Patrick and St Columba. Her father was an Irish lord named Duptace. Born c.451 of princely ancestors at Faughart, near Dundalk, County Louth; d. 1 February, 525, at Kildare, refusing many good offers of marriage, she became a nun and received the veil from St. Macaille. St Brigid and her cross are linked together by the story that she wove this form of cross at the death bed of either her father or a paganlord, who upon hearing what the cross meant, asked to be baptized. She founded a convent so that other young girls might become Nuns, Bridget made people think of the Blessed mother because she was so pure and sweet, so lovely and gentle. They called her the "Mary of the Irish".

St Patrick and St Bridget

SAINT COLUMBKILL

Saint Columcille, was born of a noble family in Donegal, Ireland, in the year 521, and was ordained a priest and monk in 546. When he was 42 years old, he was exiled from Ireland and went to Scotland. There he spent the next 34 years (establishing churches and schools) and spent much time copying the Scriptures and other manuscripts and writing poems. Columcille died in 597 and is honoured as the Parton of Scotland.

SAINT PAUL

The indefatigable Apostle of the Gentiles was converted from Judaism on the road to Damascus, where he experienced a vision of the resurrected Jesus after which he was temporarily blinded. After preaching in the synagogues that Jesus is the Christ, the Son of God, he incurred the hatred of the Jews and had to flee from the city. St Paul had a broad outlook and was perhaps endowed as the most brilliant person to carry Christianity to varied lands, such as Cyprus, Asia minor (modern Turkey), mainland Greece, Crete and Rome.

Looking to the left above the baptism font there is a small stained glass window with an inscription in memory of Patrick Scanlon. Directly opposite, a similar window states that Patrick Scanlon is buried in New York, Patrick Scanlon was born in Glentown, a townland in this Parish. As a youth he committed a minor misdemeanour. His mother took him to the priest in Doneyloop at that time to have him admonished. The priest suggested to Patrick that he should emigrate and he took that advice and went to America. In America he prospered and became a building contractor; he employed many Urney immigrants. When Doneyloop church was being built the fundraisers sent tickets to relatives who were workmen with Scanlon. When he heard of this he sent a substantial contribution. This story has been handed down through the generations.

St Columbkill and St Paul

THE SIGNIFICANCE OF THE SYMBOLS OF THE CHURCH

The Sanctuary Lamp is always lit indicating the presence of the Eucharist in the tabernacle. It is only extinguished on Holy Thursday and is relit during the Easter Vigil ceremony. The crucifix hanging above the altar reminds us to worship Christ while the windows suggest we honour our Saints. The three statures in the church are the Scared Heart of Jesus, the Virgin Mary and St Anthony of Padua.

THE STATIONS OF THE CROSS

The story of the passion and death of Christ is told in paintings around the walls of the Church from his condemnation to his rising from the dead. One of the great privileges of pilgrims to walk the Via Dela Rosa in the old city of Jerusalem when in the Holy Land. The cemetery lies to the west of the Church and has been extended twice.

THE 3 LAY ORGANISATIONS

We have three lay organisations within the Parish: St Vincent de Paul, The Legion of Mary and the Charismatic Movement St Vincent de Paul, this organisation was started by a French man named Frederick Ozanam who took as his Parton St Vincent de Paul. Its' members give their time to raising funds mainly by Church gate Collections and distribute help among the needy. Our Doneyloop conference was started by Fr Walter Hegarty in 1932.

The Legion of Mary was started by Fr William Rafferty in 1976. The members are devoted to prayerful honour of the Blessed Mary and visit the sick in hospitals and in their homes.

Fr Rafferty also founded the Charismatic Movement in 1976. The members meet weekly and their inspiration comes through meditation of Scripture, hymn singing and music and seeking inspiration from the Holy Sprit. They attract people from all denominations and have helped people afflicted by addictions.

In 2004, Fr B McGoldrick had our sanctuary area remodelled with a marble altar, celebrant's chair, lectern and tabernacle in cream and brown. We now also have a Celtic cross erected in 2006 by Fr B McGoldrick.

BOUNDARIES 1836 & TODAY

A map of Urney shows the Tyrone end of the Parish bounded Camus and Ardstraw. Now in 2011 it is Melmount and Sion Mills. The Donegal boundary remains the same Donaghmore and Clonleigh.

OTHER CLERGY

William Mac Cathmhaoil/ William MacCawell (McCall, Campbell), rector (parish priest) of Urney and dean of Derry in 1397, died before 1407.

Donatus Okerbulan/ Donchadh Ó Cearbhalláin/O'Carolan, rector of Urney 1397.

Johannes Ochasalaid/ EoinÓ Casaile (Cushley), canon of Derry, vicar resigned before1413.

Donaldus Macauhemail Ochellayd/Dónall Mac an Bhaird Ó Ceallaigh vicar provided 1413 dead by 1430. A Dónall Mac an Bhaird was deprived in 1432 for concubinage, perjury and dilapidation of parish.

Donaldus Obryn/ Dónall Ó Braoin (Breen), vicar deprived of office as curate for letting a parishioner die without the sacraments after being widely sought 1482. If proved, Aodh Ó Cearbhalláin to succeed.

Cormacus Micromnige/ Cormac Mac Con Mí (McNamee) canon of Derry, rector of Urney 1489. Florentius Mac Varde/ Fógartach Mac an Bhaird, vicar (curate) of Urney 1607.

ConnougherO Mungan/Conchúr Ó Mongáin/ Conor O' Mongan of Urney and Termon O' Mungan, was 'amongst the Cathloic clergy who were kind to non-Catholics in the area occupied by the forces besieging' Derry in 1689. This army of James II was commanded at a time by General Richard Hamilton, grandson of Sir George Hamilton, brother of the earl of Abercorn.

Parish Priests

1724	Cornelius O'Mongan
? 1735?	Fr Nugent
? - 1771	Dr Robert McCawell
1770 - 80	Bishop Phillip McDevitt
1780 – 1790?	Fr McCaul?
1790 – 1809	Arthur McHugh
1809 – 20	Charles McCaffrey
1820 – 36	Fr (Mc) Henry
1836 – 39	Neal O' Donnell
1839 – 45	Denis McDevitt
1845 – 47	Paul Bradley
1847 – 57	Michael McGlinchey
1857 – 68	Edward Mc Bride
1863 – 1903	James Connelly
1903 – 09	John McElhatton
1909 – 29	James O' Kane
1829 – 38	Hugh McGlynn

Curates

Years	Name	Years	Name
1830 – 5	William McGillen	1892 – 9	Thomas Dee
1834 – 7	John O' Flaherty	1894 – 95	Walter O'Neill
1836 – 40	Hugh Nugent	1896 – 7	Andrew Campbell
1838	Patrick McCloskey	1898 – 1903	Dennis Morris
1841 – 42	William Browne	1900 – 8	William McLaughlin
1843	Edward O' Flaherty	1904 – 9	Patrick O' Mullan
1844 – 51	John McGilligan	1906 – 7	Patrick O' H Blaney
1845	Terence P McGowan	1908 – 13	Michael Smith
1847 – 8	John Doherty	1909 – 13	James Harkin
1849 – 67	James Connolly	1910 – 14	Philip O' Doherty
1852 – 3	James McCollum	1913 – 15	Patrick O' Mullan
1854 - 6	Denis Mc Feely	1914	Hugh Smith
1857 – 64	John Mc Cullagh	1914 – 18	William Elliot
1863 – 4	Charles Mc Faul	1919 – 16	Thomas O' Doherty
1863 – 4	Michael Rogers	1916 – 20	Francis Fox
1864 – 71	Frances O' Neill	1918	Patrick J Devlin
1865 – 66	Bernard McLaughlin	1919 – 21	Joseph Devine
1867 – 71	Frances Kelly	1919 – 36	George Ryan
1872 –	Charles Kelly	1921 – 26	Michael McMenamin
1872 – 91	John McConnellogue	1922 – 4	Patrick O' Mullan
1873 – 82	Joseph O' Doherty	1925 – 38	Peadar MacLoinsigh
1881	Charles McHugh	1927 – 37	Walter Hegarty
1884 – 90	William T O' Doherty	1932 – 38	William Devine
1891 – 93	Sam Connelly	1937 – 38	John Sherrin
		1938	Joseph Tinney

In 1939, the boundaries of the Parish of Urney were re-drawn. Sion Mills and the Melmount area of Strabane formed a new independent Parish. The parish of Urney then consisted of Doneyloop and Castlederg.

Parish Priests

1939	Michael McMenamin
1962	Thomas E Devine
1974	Philip Donnelly

Curates

Years	Name	Years	Name
1939 – 40	Joseph Tinney	1949 – 52	John McGilligan
1941	Thomas Bradley	1953 – 62	Richard V Gallagher
1942 – 4	Peadar MacLoinsigh	1957 – 62	Edward Daly
1945 – 9	Michael McHugh	1960 – 64	Henry O'Neill
		1965 -76	Henry J O'Kane

Urney and Castlefin
Established in 1976. Consisting of the Doneyloop and Castlefin areas from the former Parish of Urney and Parish of Donaghmore.

Parish Priests

1976	William Rafferty
1995	Brian McGoldrick

Curates

Years	Name	Years	Name
1976 – 88	James McGonigle	993 – 95	Seamus Farrelly
1989 – 91	Kevin mullan	1995	Desmond Polke

Thanks to the writings of Fr Walter Hegarty, Fr Phillip Donnelly and Fr Kieran Devlin.

The Following are the inscriptions in Urney graveyard.
Tyrone, on the tombs of three priests who worked in the Donegal – Tyrone border parishes in 18th and 19th century.

1771
Dr Robert Mc Caul V.G.

Here lyeth the body of Rev. Robert McCaul. Doctor of Law of the University of Paris. Pastor of Urney Lifford and Camis during the space offifteen years and Vicar General of the Diocese of Derry, who departed this life in the fortieth year of his age on the 23rd day of April in the year of Our Lord, 1771. He was much esteemed in life and much regretted after death"

1808
Father James Mongan P.P.

"Here lies the remains
of Jas. Mongan,
Pastor of Strabane and Lifford,
Who departed this life
on the 9th of June,
1808, aged 47 years

1798
Hep??cn Kennedy

HIS
Here Lyth the Body of
HEP??CN KENNEDY
Who departed this life
Feb 7th 1798
Age 36 years

1838
Fr. Hugh Monaghan CC of Derry

Who Departed this life on the 23rd April 1838 aged 27 years.
His brother, James Monaghan who Departed this life on the 11th of August

1812
His Father Patrick Monaghan

Who Departed this life on the 25th September aged 67 yrs in 1842. His Mother Sarah Monaghan alis Brandin who departed this life on 7th October 1848 aged 63yrs In graveyard known as Ballybogan in the townland of Churchtown

Urney Bell

By Myles Donnelly

There have been a lot of Catholic churches built around Urney since it became semi legal again after 1780 to be a Catholic. The Bridgend and Melmount parts of Strabane were part of the parish of Urney at that time. In 1845 Urney's parish priest Fr. Paul Bradley then organized the building of a new church for the people of this part of Urney in the middle of what is now the old graveyard at Melmount road in Strabane. This original St. Mary's chapel was completed in 1846 and a curate was transferred there from the main Doneyloop church. In 1906 the parish priest Fr. McElhatton bought the lands across the road where the present Melmount church stands. The large house there became the main parochial house where Fr. McElhatton then went to live. Fr. McElhatton then had the Urney bell transferred to this main Urney church in Melmount. The bell was then set up on a stone plinth at the left entrance to the church. The inscription on it read,

Dedicated to St. Colmcille, Doneyloop, by the most Reverend Dr. Francis Kelly D.D. for the honour and service of God. This bell was erected by the most Rev. James Connolly P.P. 1869.

Siggersons CLG followers will be interested to know that the Ballycolman (including Siggerson Park), the Bridgend and the rest of Melmount were part of Urney parish up until 1938 when Urney was subdivided and the new Mourne Parish was created around St Mary's in Melmount.

The Urney Bell marked the days and events of the parish until 'The Emergency' or WW2 as the British called it. The British then started to collect scrap metals for their weapons factories in Belfast and England. They were initially asking for voluntary donations but as they began to panic in 1940 soldiers were sent out in groups to take railing and gates etc. without asking. (You can still see the remaining rusting stumps where the seized railings were cut along low walls of the Bridgend area in Strabane between the barber shop and the tyre depot). There was also talk of seizing Catholic Church bells and railings. The parish priest and local people weren't too happy about this project. The legacy of penal times was still strongly felt.

The famines were still a living memory for a few elderly people and Catholics were still considered 2nd class people by the repressive unionist government in Belfast. There had been no government help for the flooded residents of the Bridgend area of the parish in 1929.

To cut a long story short, the priest and a few local men basically dug a big hole one night in the graveyard and lowered the bell into it. The bell was extremely heavy, the work hard and it all had to be completed before dawn. The bell was to be retrieved when the threat had passed in a couple of years.

Once buried however it was 'out of sight out of mind'. Gradually the bell faded from memory probably helped by the increasingly shocking news of various events from the war in the papers and on the radio and closer to home too at times.

In the late 1950's Fr Convery the new parish priest of Melmount was becoming puzzled about the empty plinth. He eventually found out about the now almost forgotten bell but no one knew where it was. Records were searched but no mention of it could be found (the earlier priest and his men had done their job well). While he was out walking one day through the graveyard the parish priest encountered an old man who was strolling around visiting graves and they got to talking about this and that. As they were about to part ways the old man smiled and asked the priest if he'd had any luck locating the old bell yet. 'Not really' replied the priest 'It could be anywhere around here' The old man rubbed his chin thoughtfully and ventured 'Suppose Father you've looked in the old grave records?' 'I've been through them a fair few times now without success' the priest replied before adding 'Why do you know something?' 'Well Father....' the old man said, 'I was thinking that well... maybe...it might be a good idea to start with the one marked A Bell.

After another night of activity in the graveyard the old Urney bell was lifted and taken to a secure location and mostly forgotten about again.

The new church was built for the growing parish in 1970 and the old one was demolished. As the new flat church didn't have a bell tower it would have seemed normal for it not have a bell.

When Fr Anthony Mulvey arrived as parish priest in June 1978 he wanted to improve things for the local people. He was very pro active. He opened the boot of a 'bomb scare car' in Ballycolman one night so that the RUC would allow people to return to their homes. Another time he entered a flat complex that was surrounded and under siege by British forces (including the SAS) to help the armed occupants give themselves up without being harmed. As you would expect from a man of God he always spoke out against violence. Graffiti was painted on the chapel walls one night but removed by others later in the morning. He would receive many anonymous hate calls on the phone. His housekeeper who was from Leitrim would often have to answer the phone in his absence and would tell the crank callers to wash out their mouths with soap. He organized the building (using local workers) of the extensive Melmount playing fields to complete with handball alley, bowling green, soccer pitch and the then state of the art all weather Gaelic pitch with concrete stand (the first in Strabane). Shamrocks Hurling Club used this as their home ground and training pitch for years until it was bulldozed to make way for Holy Cross College in 2008. The large Melmount Centre was also built using all local labour. This was the premier entertainment venue in the area attracting many of the best bands going as well as providing dozens of jobs. He set up the Melmount Community Care which employed over 120 local people at one time and he began pushing for a by/pass to take the Derry/Letterkenny to Dublin traffic away from the Parish.

He was however missing one detail, a bell for the church. After a few inquiries about buying a new bell Fr. Mulvey was approached quietly and told that there was no need as the parish already had one. This time the bell was easier to find and Fr. Mulvey was taken to see it. A go ahead man like himself was probably wondering why no one had already put it up but he said nothing and started organizing the work. He had a new stand built to the left of the chapel and the whole thing was blessed and being a progressive person he had it automated. The bell was then rung for the first time in 45 years in front of a large crowd. Manys a 1st Communion, Confirmation or Wedding photo has been taken in front of it since. While some would argue that the bell should be returned to Doneyloop it is worth pointing out that it was replaced with an even bigger one.

Alt Presbyterian Church

By George Harper

In 1833 there was no church in Alt and Presbyterians worshiped in the surrounding parishes of Donaghmore, Urney and Ardstraw. The Rev Andrew Maxwell was minster of the session church in Castlederg and also preached at Drumlegagh near Ardstraw. In 1833 it was reported to the session synod, the Presbytery of Donegal that the Castlederg part of his charge had become a separate congregation. At the same meeting, Mr Samuel Stewart, a member of Rev. Maxwell's congregation, was licensed to preach the gospel and it was also reported that a respectable number of people in Alt had requested 'a supply of sermon'. Mr Stewart was put in charge of the new congregation in Alt and in 1834 it was reported that Mr. Stewart had accepted a call from Alt, where he was ordained on 30th July 1834. With the new congregation needing a place of worship, Rev. Stewart quickly got to work and in 1835 a new seeders meeting-house was erected and in a message to the session synod he noted "his hopes had been realised and that the congregation was flourishing".

Alt Presbyterian Church

Around this time, Rev Stewart obtained a farm and Cottage in Alt, for a yearly rent of £27 and 10 shillings.

The success of Alt Church did not go unnoticed, as The Synod of Ulster set up a rival congregation at the Raws, about ½ mile from Alt, and on 30th November 1836, the Rev Hutcheson Perry was installed as its Minister. Rev. Perry did not have much success and was soon on his way to preach at Portglenone.

The Union of Synods in 1840 brought the Presbyterian Synods together as 'General Assembly of the Presbyterian Church in Ireland' and from then on Alt became known as Alt Presbyterian Church. In 1843 Rev Stewart had a new school house built which was placed under the National board of Education. After a long and successful Ministry lasting over 47 years Rev. Stewart retired from active duty on 3rd October 1881.

Alt's next Minister was the Rev James Knox, where he was installed on the 3rd of January 1882. Rev Knox was a very progressive man when it came to the church buildings. In 1886 the church was renovated and on the 3rd of November was re-opened by the Rev. Dr. Whigham, then moderator of the general Assembly. In 1891, a session room was built and in 1899, the church was enlarged and the church grounds were opened as a Cemetery. Before this, members of the congregation were buried mostly in the surrounding cemeteries of Urney and Donaghmore

In 1900, Mr William Cooper, a ruling Elder for over 40 years passed away and soon afterwards it was decided to choose additional Elders. On the 28th February 1901 Messrs J.B. Gamble, J.P. Robert Harper, Hugh Cooper and Robert Brooks were installed as members of session.

By this time the school of 1843 was in such a poor condition it was decided to build a new school. This was built in 1902. Despite the best efforts of Rev Knox, to keep the church building in good condition, it was decided in 1911 to have the church almost entirely rebuilt. Pitch pine was used on the ceiling and a hot water heating system using pipes was installed which was very modern for its day. A stained glass window in memory of Mrs Knox who passed away in 1906 was also installed. By the time the renovation was complete, nearly £600 pounds had been spent.

One of Ireland's most historic documents, The Ulster Covenant and the Ulster Declaration was signed in Alt Church on the 28th of September 1912. The first organ for the church was purchased in October 1917 at a cost of £20.

By 1920 Alt had a large committee looking after its affairs:

John James Martin	Alic Crilly
Tom Roulston	Wm Mc Kay
Thomas Temple	Robert Taylor
Archie Kemps	David Porter
John Blackburn	Hamilton Baxtor
John Blackburn	Wm Browne
David Thompson	Tom Barr
Oliver Campbell	David Mc Clintock
Thomas Mortland	Robert Mc Kane
Tom Carson	Joseph Cooper
John Crilly	Andrew Donnell
Wm Crilly	

The Session was: J.B. Gamble, Harper, Brooks and Rev. Knox.

The Rev. James Johnston was installed in 1924 for a short stay of four years followed by Rev. Thomas Mc Candless from 1928 until 1942. During this time the church was kept in good repair despite the fact Ireland was in an "economic war" with England, the world was in a "great depression" and in 1939 entered a period of World War. The Forth minster in Alt was Rev. James Herman Browne who had a short stay of a few months before Rev. R.G. Doherty was installed in September 1942 spending fourteen years in Alt until 1956.

Rev. J. Sproule was the next minster in charge staying in Alt for ten years. It was during his time the new school across the road from the church was built. It was opened in 1960 with Mrs Hutchinson the teacher at that time. There were three ministers from 1966 until 1983, Rev. George Preston 1966-1972, Rev. A.B.R. Clarke

1972-1973 and Rev. W.J Patterson from 1973 until 1983. During Rev. Patterson's time a new organ and new furnishings for the church were purchased. The Rev. Stewart Jones was installed in 1985 the year of the 150th anniversary of Alt church. This was a busy time with the anniversary celebrated on the 9th of October. The Rev. E Henning looked after the congregation from 1988 until 1991. In 1990 the Church building was refurbished with many members of the congregation helping out.

Alt Upper National School Built in 1902.

In 1992 Alt Church after 157 years with the Donegal presbytery moved to the Strabane and Derry presbytery sharing the minister with second Castlederg Presbyterian Church. Alt's new minister was Rev. R. Graham until 1998. Rev. Roy Caston was with Alt until 2005. The Church was also re-roofed in 2005. The present minister is Rev. John Honeyford with Alt and Second Presbyterian Church Castlrderg since 2007. Alt Presbyterian Church has now been in existence one hundred and seventy six years. Although the congregation is small in number, the congregation remember with pride, the passion and determination of Mr Samuel Stewart and his congregation of 1835 and look forward to Alt's next big anniversary in 2035.

Renovation at Alt Presbyterian Church 1990

By Isobel Roulston

Members of Alt congregation started the challenging and indeed daunting task of refurbishing their church building during the first week of January 1990. What follows is a brief account of the work involved:

The church contained a total of sixteen pews, each nineteen feet long and extremely heavy. The heating system was dismantled. The Brass Lamps were taken down and packed away for safe-keeping.

Trees from the local forest were sawed and used as jibs to hold the scaffolding for the next step of removing the old plaster from the walls. The youth of the congregation worked with jack-hammers for several days cleaning up and removing the rubble. Experts in Damp Proofing were called in and while they worked on the church walls, Deva Porter and Jim Crilly cut the pews in two. The pews and all the panelling were then sent to Buncrana to be stripped of 150 years of old varnish and polish.

The windows were removed, leaving the building in a sorry state indeed. Would it be possible to put it all together again? February was a very cold and wet, and anxious thoughts at the enormity of the task filled most peoples' minds. We reminded ourselves that God was by our side and we knew that we needn't be afraid. John and Thomas Campbell then started the tedious job of plastering.

On the 1st May the new PVC windows arrived and were fitted. This was an uplifting day for the congregation who could see things slowly beginning to take shape. The plastering continued and was completed by the end of April. Repairs were made to the floor and joists. It was then re-sheeted. The platform was then erected at the front of the church. To facilitate this, the pulpit had to be raised, this was no easy task as it necessitated a great deal of care and thought.

The next step was to re-design the back panelling and change the two doors. Previously there were two very narrow side aisles, the new plan was to have a centre aisle. Due to its size, it was not possible to move the partition out for stripping so the members of the congregation took on the task of stripping the old varnish.

When this was completed the woodwork had to be hand sanded. The side panels were replaced.

Repairs to the electrical work were carried out. New spot lights were mounted in the ceiling to boost the light given by the old oil lamps.

In June the task of sanding and placing the pews took place. Stepping the pews back at the front of the church was a great idea as this gave more room and also gave more emphasis to the pulpit. The congregation were delighted to find that after removing the black paint from the banisters of the pulpit, they found pitch pine wood which was the same as the rest of the wood in the church.

The decorative border caused a problem but with some wallpaper, gold paint and a lady's time, this problem was overcome and now stands as a credit to her and to the church.

In July the unseen jobs such as the sanding, staining, sealing and lacquering the small boards under the pews started. It is reckoned that each of the 1,000 boards were handled at least ten times from beginning to end. The church was then painted. At the end of July the last major job began, the staining of the pews, all the panelling and the pulpit.

In August the upholstering of the pulpit, replacing of the glass depicting a view from the church in the centre doors. The choosing and laying of the carpet, the hanging of the lamps, the painting and the cleaning inside and out were among the last tasks to be completed.

On the 2nd September 1990, eight months from beginning to end, after a very challenging experience, happy and anxious times, major and minor decisions taken, with a very rewarding ending, the congregation of the Alt Presbyterian Church celebrated their opening service at 7pm.

Urney - History / People / Place

Christ Church, Urney

By Christina Speers

RECTORS

1401	William MacKathmayl
1401	Donalus O'Keruolan
1432	Donald Macabaird O'Cellaid
1433	John O'Cearbollan
1535	Toroletus Mc Aeed
1617	Isaac Wood
1638	William Kingsmill
1657	James Wallace
1661	Vacant
1662	Thomas Buttolph
1672-1701	John Leslie
1701-1729	David Jenkins
1729-1740	Robert Downes
1740-1768	William Henry
1768-1780	(Hon) William Beresford
1780-1789	William Foster
1789-1794	Hon. John Pomeroy
1794-1813	Robert Fowler
1813-1814	Hon. Charles Knox
18141835	James Jones – buried at Urney
1835-1849	Robert Hume
1849-1862	Benjamin Bloomfield Gough
1862	Charles Seymour
1872-1898	Thomas Olphert
1899-1921	John Olphert – Canon
1921-1953	Richard Scandrett
1953-1967	William E. Davey
1968-1984	Gerald J.A. Carson - Canon
1986-1992	Raymond Thompson
1992-1998	John I. H. Stafford
1999-2006	David Skuce
2007-	Raymond McKnight

CURATES

1622	Curate unnamed "MA" and a preacher
1665	John Sinclair
1677	John Monroe
1680	Andrew Leslie M.A.
1692	William Knox
1699	David Allardice
-1735	John Browne
1768	Robert Magee
1777	Jocelyn Ingram
1786	John Beresford Hill
1796	Archibald Hamilton
1811	Thomas Ellison
1814-1832	Robert Scott
1828	Edward Atkinson
1835	John Conroy
1847	Vincent B. Smith
1862	John Alexander Stewart
1864	Joseph Rawlins
1865	Henderson Baldwin Mason
1866-1872	Richard Bennett
1880-1883	George Gillington
1895-1899	Alexander Thomas Kilpatrick
1919-1921	Richard Scandrett

VICARS

1413	John O'Cahsalad
1413	Donald Mackhabaird
1428	John O'Cassalay
1430	Donald Macauhemail
1430	Roger O'Gurmileadgaydh (O'Gormley)
1482	Donald O'Bryn
1482	Odo O'Ceruolan
1535	Odo Macabaird

Additional information;

- 1535 Magonius O'Gormley, Toroletus McCaogha and Velanus O'Cerbulan claim The Vicarage of Urney.
- William Henry -   promised, 1768, to every man a Bible and a broadsword to defend it, and to every woman a Prayer Book and a Spinning wheel.
- 1768 (Hon) William Beresford – later Bishop of Dromore.
- 1780 William Foster – later Bishop of Cork
- 1794 Robert Fowler – later Bishop of Ossory
- 1813 (Hon) Charles Knox – He was father of Primate Knox

The word Urney means Oratory – a place for private prayer and worship. Many worshippers and visitors comment upon the ambience of the interior of the Church and the aura of peace experienced within its walls. Designed by Welland and Gillespie, Christ Church, built in 1865, and consecrated in 1866 replaced the church of 1723. The remains of the latter, still standing in the graveyard, provide the hallowed resting place of local families including Herdman, Goslin, Ferrier, McCormick, Wallace, Baird, Adams, Perry, Colquohoun and Harris.

Christ Church is a cruciform building with a polygonal apse. On the north side is a tower surmounted by a spire. There is a five sided apsidal chancel. In the west gable is a beautiful rose window through which the setting sun reflects its colours along the aisle. In the south wall are three windows of two lights, two of which are of clear glass and the third is of stained glass in memory of James Baird 1894. Part of the south wall is recessed behind two arches.

The north aisle has two clear windows of two lights. There are five stained glass windows in the sanctuary. The first two depict "on earth peace good will towards men" and "truly this was the son of God" and commemorate those who fell in the Great War. The middle window depicts the text " I will not leave you comfortless" while the two on the right depict the texts "I ascend onto my father and your father" and " I am he that liveth and was dead", both of which are in memory of John Coloquhoun of Castletown House who died 1901.

Christ Church, Urney. 2011

The baptistery window depicts a dove and a cross and is in memory of John Patrick Herdman who died in 1987. The Herdman family is world famous for the production of linen thread for people in all walks of life including residents of the Vatican and of Buckingham Palace.

The pulpit is in memory of Thomas Olphert, Dean of Derry and Rector of Urney 1872-1898. Two prayer desks commemorate John Herdman who died in 1903. The Bible reposes on a majestic brass eagle lectern. The tiling in the chancel is in memory of Andrew Ferguson Knox who died in 1878 (great-grand-father of Ian Perry, Urney Park). Panelling around the sanctuary is in memory of John Herdman 1906. The two manual Conacher organ was given by Joseph Keterson, Toronto (also donor of a bell) in 1889.

On the west wall is a monument to Sir James Galbraith, Urney Park, who died 1827. On the north wall is a memorial to William Stewart M.D. who died in 1851 and to his wife and sons. A brass memorial commemorates Lila Ferrier, and another one, Brigadier General Tom Pearse who died in 1947. On the north aisle are memorials to Olive Colquhoun, to James Jones, Rector of Urney, 1814-1835, who is buried in the local graveyard, to Benjamin Fenton, who died in 1804, and to William Maxwell who died 1789. On the south wall, John Olphert Rector of Urney 1899-1921, is commemorated. He died in 1923. There is also a brass memorial to Kenneth Smyth who died in 1971.

At the end of the eighteenth century, the rectory was destroyed by fire. Legend has it that the Rector, the Rev. Robert Fowler, who later became Bishop of Ossory, was dining with friends close by when the butler rushed in with the news. "Let it burn" said Mr Fowler, and continued to enjoy his dinner. Later he applied to the Ecclesiastical Commissioners for financial aid to build a new rectory. His remarks had reached the ears of the Commissioners and they replied that as he had said "Let it burn" they would say "Let you build" and turned down his request. He was very annoyed and said, "I will – and I will build one of 3 or more storeys with 34 rooms", and he did so. His very large rectory was sold in 1919 and became a factory producing confectionery which bore the name Urney. Later it was destroyed by fire.

With the erection of the flax-spinning mill by the Herdman family and a Mr Mulholland three and a half miles over the hill, a new church, St Saviours, was built to accommodate 130 people in the growing village of Sion Mills. This church was never consecrated because it was too small for the increasing congregation. Due to the initiative of the then Rector, Canon J. Olphert, backed by Brigadier General Ambrose St Quentin Ricardo, CMG, CBE, DSO, of the Royal Inniskilling Fusiliers, another splendid church was built. It was dedicated on 15th May 1909 and known as the Church of the Good Shepherd. This church was modelled on a church in Pistoia near Florence, and is a fine example of the Italian style of architecture. The architect was W. F. Unsworth.

THE BELLS OF CHRIST CHURCH, URNEY

At the north-west side of the church there is a square tower with an octagonal brooch spire. In it there is a small "five minutes" bell, which is 18" in diameter, sounding the note A, and beautifully decorated. It has cannons, and is inscribed

S. DOMINGO DEGVSMAN
SOLANOME FACIT EN SVLLA AN DE 1734

The bell was cast in Seville, Spain and, as was the custom in Roman Catholic countries, it was given the name St. Domingo. The churchwarden of the day was responsible for the bell coming to Urney Church in 1744.

There is also a large bell, 40 ½ ", in diameter, weighing 12 cwts, sounding the note G. It has cannons, and is inscribed as follows:

```
            J MURPHY FOUNDER DUBLIN
              GLORIA IN EXCELSIS DEO
               EX DONO JOS KETERSON
                   TORONTO 1890
          THOS OLPHERT M.A.  CANON RECTOR
      E.C. HERDMAN              CHURCHWARDENS
        J E SHARKIE                          URNEY
```

On the opposite side of the waist there is the standard Murphy stamp, consisting of the harp, with crown above it, which, in 1891, according to a correspondent at the time of the bell's installation, is emblematic of "Ireland united with England under the rule of our gracious Queen, which state of things may God long preserve."

The Baptistery

Originally the Baptistery was to the right immediately within the west door.
When Lady Herdman, our talented organist, reluctantly retired, due to advancing years, she was succeeded by Miss Fanny Elliott, the organist in the Church of the Good Shepherd, Sion Mills and she travelled with the Rector of Urney, to our service at 12 o'clock. Miss Elliott died very suddenly at her home immediately after a service in Sion Mills.

It was then that Mrs Davey, our Rector's wife, utilised the resources within Christ Church – i.e. the wives of Dai Baird, of Tom Baird and of Sammy Shannon, plus Betty Wilson and Hall Speers. The newly acquired organists, accustomed to their choir members directly around them, could not hear the choir who sat in pews to the right of the organ. It was decided to move the font across the aisle to the floor space at the organ and fill the font space with pews from the north aisle – a very successful operation except that the floor, not reinforced, was sinking beneath the weight of the font. The problem was sorted by transferring the heavy font from the west door to the stone floor inside the south door – not an ideal situation.

Years later, the Rev G.J. A Carson, later to become Canon of Derry Cathedral, had the stone font from the 1723 church in the graveyard, transferred to its present site inside the north door – a very happy arrangement. Of necessity, the font in three parts, i.e. base, stem and bowl, was laid in a local farmyard where it was thoroughly cleaned (in those days hens, geese, ducks and turkeys roamed freely). One hen, evidently wanting to outdo the swallows in Psalm 84, laid her egg in the font bowl. Perhaps there's seed for a sermon!! Later the Rev. John Stafford remarked that the font did not have a lid. We are indebted to Fred Buick who fashioned a most appropriate lid out of wood salvaged from Mosley Linen Mill. Recently, the font area has been greatly enhanced by the gift of pew cushions in memory of Mrs. Mary Donnell from her husband John Donnell, Finn View.

Clergymen within living memory
Rev. Richard Scandrett
The Rev. Richard Scandrett was curate from 1919-1921, and Rector from 1921-1953. He will be remembered as a saintly, sweetly spoken man ministering to a church packed full of people – with no lighting except at Christmas and Easter Holy Communion Services at 8.30 am when parishioners provided candleholders to supplement the single oil lamp hanging in the Sanctuary – plus two silver candle holders, the property of the Rector.

Mrs Scandrett, although suffering from multiple sclerosis, was organist in the Church of the Good Shepherd and bravely, probably painfully, climbed the steps to the choir in the gallery. Upon retirement, they lived in a small house in the village.

The Rev. R. Scandrett died in Belfast, leaving a son, Michael. Once, I expect upon the brink of a well-earned holiday, he wrote the following for the Mid Ulster Magazine:-

Hurrah for the sea and the sky
Hurrah for the breeze and the bay
To Urney and Sion "Goodbye"
I'm off for a long holiday (at last two weeks minus a day)

The old church in Urney graveyard built in 1723

Rev. William Edwin Davey

In 1953, the Rev. Edwin Davey came from Culmore, Co. Derry, with his wife Fan, their two sons Brian and Myles and their daughter Sheelagh. They took up residence in the new Rectory at Melmount Road, which was a much smaller building than it is today. Of necessity the dining room was extended resulting in a larger bedroom upstairs.

Soon a large Branch of The Mothers Union and Young Wives was established, as well as other Youth Organisations. Those members who did not have obligatory jobs during the day often catered for local Cricket matches and various functions, all for fund-raising.

The heating came through a grid in the centre aisle from a furnace below (a pleasure to stand there on cold mornings) and was tended by our Sexton, Jimmy Logan . Under the guidance of our new Rector, a party of volunteers from Urney, joined by skilled volunteers from Sion Mills, installed central heating in Christ Church, building a new furnace area to accommodate the necessary equipment. The cost was approximately £800. Electricity was installed for £300. Half of the cost of this was borne by Mr. Q.Y. Lawson MBE who later paid for the installation of Calor Gas in our church hall – better known as Lower Urney School. The Urney parishioners deeply appreciated the skilled work of the volunteers from Sion Mills. This was followed by a great orgy of scrubbing and washing the pews and floors – again helped by the women of Sion Mills. Jokes and camaraderie took the toil out of the hard work. Water had to be brought from the well beside Laurence Byrne's, and transported in creamery cans on Laurence's donkey-drawn cart, ably pushed by Laurence and the Rector.

During the Daveys' sojourn with us, Bishop Tyndall presided in 1966 over a Missionary society initiative, *Mutual Responsibility and Interdependence in the Body of our Lord*, MRI. The Rev. Edwin Davey, accompanied by his wife, was appointed to represent the Dioceses of Derry and Raphoe in Jamaica. While there, we understand that they visited the area where an Urney parishioner, Andrew Sproule (Tullymoan) worked. He is remembered for leaving in his will £1000 to Urney Parish – the interest to be donated to the Poor of the Parish. It is said that on Easter morning, Andrew Sproule found a starving woman by the roadside, and took her home to his mother who treated her to a boiled egg. At Easter in those days, everyone ate as many eggs as they wished! Children often went around farm houses begging for eggs so that they could have a feast on Easter Day.

Not all money came to Urney Parish. Four years after Andrew's death, the money had not arrived. An emissary was sent to Jamaica – the Rector and Churchwardens becoming uneasy, suspecting that Mr. Sproule's estate had been mismanaged. Today there is a small income used as requested. Bishop Gibson, a native of Jamaica, with his two sisters, visited our Parish as guests of the Daveys. A social evening was held in their honour and our Mothers' Union Branch donated to them £20 (all our funds) towards the building of a new church. Also, to welcome the Daveys safely home, a social evening was held in the Recreation Hall to which all the interested clergy – those in charge of the parish during their absence, and all our own parishioners came. One fact remains in memory – the harrowing description of the storm at sea when they knelt in their cabin and prayed for a safe landing.

Mrs. Fan Davey, a zealous church worker, gave of her musical talent as organist when necessary and as conductor of choir practices. She was keenly interested in drama, making sure that the Mothers' Union members performed sketches at the annual party in Urney Church Hall. The sketches were hilarious, the preparation, and evenings were fun, whether practising in the Rectory or in members' homes. Youth

Organisations were encouraged. The local Cancer Research Campaign started in the Rectory when Mrs. Davey, at the request of Major General F.L. Tottenham, hosted the inaugural meeting. Collectors were organised to visit every home in the village and surrounding countryside.

The Wells Organisation addressed parochial Fund Raising. The parish had a huge sit-down meal in the Recreation Hall when every home was represented and heard addresses from the Rector and chosen speakers including Treasurer and Secretary. Above all, the Daveys like their successors, were a hard-working couple, and were especially comforters to the sick and dying.

Reverend Gerald James Alexander Carson
The Rev. G.J.A. Carson with his wife, Sheila, came in 1968 from Dunfanaghy to Urney. A talented artist in oils, he is famous for his paintings. In this Diocese he will be remembered for his contribution of sketches of the many churches in the historical Diocesan Publication entitled *In His Hand 1870 – 1970*, the proceeds from the sale of which went to Christian Aid.

He was appointed to the post of Press Officer by Bishop Eames and later became Editor of *The Diocesan News* under Bishop J. Mehaffey, where his artistic ability was often put to good use. He continued with the many organisations inherited from his predecessor and added a new dimension with Art classes. Also, he held discussion groups following evening services during Lent, plus a bible study group series.

His incumbency was not without sorrow. Kenneth Smyth, recently married to Joan, was assassinated at Tullymoan. Our Church Hall suffered minor damage when a device was thrown through the kitchen window. After voluntary repair by our own members, we continued to use the building for Church functions, even for church services when Christ Church was under repair. Later, the roof was blown off causing severe damage. The premises were sold. Now the Youth of Christ Church has no church recreation area.

More pain was experienced by the Rev. Canon G.J.A. Carson, his wife and their son Mark, when the Rectory at Sion Mills suffered severe bomb damage, leaving the house uninhabitable. Parish work operated from the home of their friends in

Taughboyne Rectory who provided temporary accommodation. Eventually Canon G.J.A.Carson was appointed Rector of Warrenpoint from which, in due course, he retired to Coleraine. Sadly, Mrs. Carson's health deteriorated. She spent her final years in a Nursing Home. Her remains are interred in a beautiful spot by the sea, at Killult in Co. Donegal. Everyone will remember with profound admiration, Canon Carson's daily visits to his beloved Sheila throughout her illness. Mrs. Carson was appointed Hon. Mothers' Union Diocesan Literature representative for our Dioceses and later became the All Ireland Representative, a position she still held in Warrenpoint.

A memorial to Sheila Carson is the local branch of the Womens' World Day of Prayer, formed in 1976, which embraces six churches; Doneyloop, St. Theresa's; Urney Presbyterian Church; Sion Mills Presbyterian Church; The Church of the Good Shepherd, Sion Mills and Christ Church, Urney. Present members respectively are: Betty Nelis, Jean Doherty, Peggy McGlinchey (Mrs. Frances O'Flaherty was the first representative from Doneyloop) Caroline Coyle, Mary Doherty, Edith Martin, June Henderson, Joyce Adams, Dorothy Smith, Daphne Sayers, Celia Ferguson, Maggie Hamilton, Christina Speers.

A report of our Womens' World Day of Prayer would be incomplete without the recollection of the Candlelight Vigil on 27th August 1998 at 8pm in the Church Square at Sion Mills in remembrance of the victims and families of the Omagh bomb. It was painful, precious and pleasing to have a stranger locked in embrace, tell us her tragic tale. Also from the Womens' World Day of Prayer was born at Edith Martin's suggestion, *the Bible Study Group* which has met in various venues and now has a permanent venue with Celia Ferguson at Braewood and is managed by Coleman Turley.

Reverend Raymond Thompson
In 1986, the Rev. Raymond Thompson, his wife Betty and son, Mark arrived. They celebrated the end of their first year with a Flower Festival in the Church of the Good Shepherd.

During their incumbency, "The Strawberry Fair" – a Saturday afternoon of shows, games, competitions, fancy dress parade, "Miss Sion Mills" etc. was started, with the consumption of lots of strawberries and cream. This has now become an annual enjoyable event involving a lot of organisation by many people, resulting in an annual financial return for church funds and a few charities.

By 1990 the Rectory had yet again to be restored following a further severe bomb attack on 15 January. An additional room was added, large enough to accommodate committee meetings. All the organisations continued with Mrs. Thompson become Enrolling Member of the Mothers' Union in succession to Christina Speers. Mrs. Thompson had the ability to play the organ which was much appreciated. From our Mothers' Union Diocesan Link we had a visit from the Rev. Doris Penina Enyaru from Uganda, on her way to London. She addressed two Diocesan Meetings and returned home with monetary and other gifts including a sewing machine. After six years, the Thompson family went to Irvinestown.

Reverend John Stafford
In 1992 we welcomed the Rev. John Stafford, to spend the last six years of his active ministry, as Rector of Urney Parish. An experienced clergyman, he was also Prebendary of Talplestone in the Diocese of Down. His wife Moira took a keen interest in the work of Mothers' Union and the Ladies' Guild, organising the invitation of ladies from the Drop-in-Centre in the village, to the Mothers' Union Christmas Lunch. Sadly Mrs. Stafford's health began to give cause for concern, and it was with great sadness that we attended her funeral Service in the Church of the Good Shepherd at the end of January 1995.

Our people particularly valued the quality of the Rev. J. Stafford's teaching sermons, and his devout conducting of Bible study groups during the week. He was assiduous in the observance of the days and weeks making up Liturgical Year and he particularly appreciated the beauty of the distinctive and very different forms of architecture as the setting of our worship. He greatly appreciated the ongoing effort made to maintain the structure and decoration of each building –Christ Church Urney and the Church of the Good Shepherd, together with the fine smaller gem that once was St.Saviour's, and which is now is the parochial hall.

We saw Mr. Stafford backing up work among the young people with particular interest in Sunday Schools, Confirmation preparation, Primary School instruction, including regular trips out to Tullywhisker. He fully encouraged those involved in the interdenominational task of getting teenagers over to visit families in the USA, at a period when the Province was far from being peaceful. Indeed it was most pleasing to see him look fresh and vigorous, when he attended the impressive Centenary Service, during 2009 in Sion Mills.

Reverend David Skuce
In 1999 the Rev. David Skuce came from Drumholm, Kilbarron and Rossnowlagh. All the church activities carried on, with perhaps more interest in Youth. It became apparent that the buildings required attention and with help from the Heritage Lottery Fund, the roof of Christ Church was repaired. All the stonework, including the spire, was sand-blasted, changing the grey coloured edifice to a sandy shade. To help pay for this, the parishioners were obliged to sell the sexton's house adjacent to the church.

At Sion Mills, a new dwelling to house the oil tank and other equipment was erected convenient to the Church Hall – the latter had a "facelift", plus the replacement of the porch by a larger porch with toilet facilities for the disabled. A Flower Festival was held. A Christmas Bazaar took place and it now has become an annual event.

The Rev. David Skuce has gone to be Rector of Maguiresbridge and Derrybrusk in Co. Fermanagh in the Diocese of Clogher. He is the son of the Ven. Francis John Leonard Skuce, former Archdeacon of Clogher.

Reverend T Raymond McKnight
At present our Rector is the Rev. Raymond McKnight who has a grown up family, two sons and two daughters and his wife Fiona.

He continues assiduously with the various organisations and has been responsible for the two Folk Exhibitions – the second to celebrate the Centenary of the Church of the Good Shepherd. The centenary service on 15th May 2009 was addressed by the Bishop of Derry and Raphoe, the Rt. Rev. Ken Good. Present were former Rectors, the Rev'ds R. Thompson, J. Stafford and D. Skuce, as well as Sheelagh Holmes, daughter of the late Rev. W. E. Davey.

Mr. McKnight has overseen the re-roofing of the Church of the Good Shepherd. Mrs McKnight, a conscientious worker, is Branch Leader of the Mothers' Union in succession to Ria Wilson, and President of the Ladies Guild, as well as being one of the organists.

Again he continues with the various organisations and has raised a great awareness of "Life during the Last Century" by organising a Folk Exhibition in the Church Hall and a more detailed exhibition in the spacious exhibition area at the Mill.

In Christ Church a new carpet has been fitted, chairs and tables provided for the Sunday school children plus a supply of catering equipment i.e. cups, saucers, boilers. Without a church hall we are obliged to serve tea in the church.

Faces synonymous with jobs at Christ Church today.
One person who stands out is Betty Wilson who has been organist since the late 1960s, sharing the duty with the late Molly Baird, Margaret Shannon and Meta Baird and occasionally Hall Speers, until they retired and she played permanently, not just on Sundays but for weddings, funerals with no salary offered. It was with great satisfaction that when Betty retired in 2009, she was presented with a large television set.

In earlier years, Betty was a Sunday School Teacher. During the years, while and since the Rev. G.J.A. Carson was here, she has been President of The Ladies Guild – organising its functions especially the annual Daffodil Tea and the Coffee Mornings for Macmillan Cancer Care. She has travelled many miles distributing notices of church events, and found time to organise donations for supper after our Harvest Thanksgiving Services etc. Sadly Betty died on Tuesday 8th March 2011.
Another stalwart voluntary worker is Harold Shannon who, with Roy Brown and Archie Baird sees to grass-mowing and the generally tidy appearance of the grounds. However, Harold also opens the church as required and keeps an eye to detail.

There are two Sunday School Teachers: - at present Mrs Olive Baird assisted by Miss Olivia Baird and Carol Galbraith, as well as members of "Safeguarding Trust".

There are Voluntary Cleaners of Today and Yesterday: - There's "The Brass" which Maggie Hamilton has undertaken for many years and is now the responsibility of Julie Ann Reid and Carol Galbraith who maintain its brilliant lustre.

And there's Ann Buick, for many years Sunday School Superintendent and Secretary to the Select Vestry, who keeps an eye on things, i.e. checking the water for flowers, especially for Festivals. She always has a welcome smile and a few words of greeting to make us all feel sociable.

And there's the role of the voluntary cleaners who keep the building clean, and there are the flower arrangers who add to the beauty. Above all there are Laurence and Heather Byrne who hold the church keys for those who need entry to the building. It's impossible adequately to thank them for their ever hospitable pleasant reception when we call - thanks to both.

And there are Members of the Select Vestry over the years including the Secretary (presently Noel McCallan) and Treasurers (presently George Hamilton and Alan Bresland) who see to the finances and fabric of the parish

And, of course, there are you in the pew for you all work together to keep A PLACE OF PRAYER – to thank our Heavenly Father for all our gifts inherited from our ancestors.

Snippets - Past and present

Mrs Cecil Frances Alexander (1818-1895), the great hymn writer is reputed to have been introduced to her husband in Urney Rectory.

James Wallace, Carricklee, who died on 10the February 1889, bequeathed £6,000 to the Deserving Protestant Poor of Urney Parish.

Around 1899 – 1900, concerts held in Urney School were reported in the Strabane Weekly News – "all very enjoyable" with familiar names of artistes including Frances and Eadie Perry who are deserving of much praise – their able performance as violinists being particularly praiseworthy. Joe Scarffe, a resident of Clady, proposed a vote of thanks.

Miss Frances Perry, on her way home in the dark, from Strabane, walked through flood water up to her waist at Flushtown Bridge and had to carry her bicycle – possibly to save her carbide lamp from extinction.

In the 1960s, it was reported that mill workers in Sion Mills could buy their houses for the price of a television.

In January 2011 Dr Catherine McKnight, daughter of Rev. R McKnight, went to Kajiado Diocese in Kenya to work as a paediatrician.

Due to temperatures of − 18 degrees C on 20th December 2010, Christ Church suffered a lot of frost damage.

Sons of the Parish of Urney who have been ordained

Rev. Caldwell Darragh; formerly of Innisclan, trained in Edinburgh, Faith Mission College, was ordained in Castlefinn, and is now the President of The Faith Mission in the British Isles.

Rev. Noel Darragh; Caldwell's brother trained at Emmanuel College, Birkenhead and was ordained in Straid Presbyterian Church where he spent 30 years, is officially retired but is still preaching in various churches.

Rev. Canon Hall Speers; currently, Rector of Barnet, North London and Canon of Antananarivo Catherdral in Madagascar, where he worked for 10 years as a missionary and Principal of the Anglican Theological College, before returning to take up duty at Folkingham, Lincolnshire.

Give us to-day our daily bread
and forgive our trespasses,
for thine is the Kingdom and the power and the glory.
Amen.

Urney Presbytarian Church

By William Haire

Scottish Presbyterians had been arriving in ULSTER since 1630 onwards but had no regular established buildings for worship. The native Irish clans the O'Neills and the O'Donnells were unhappy with this conquest of their lands by the English, who had encouraged the Presbyterians to transplant here in numbers to displace the original land owners from their native birthright.

As a result of this the clan leaders and their followers rose up in armed rebellion, which became a civil war in 1642 when English and Presbyterians were slaughtered in numbers. A regiment of Laganeers under the command of Robert and William Stewart who owned forts at Newtownstewart in County Tyrone and Kilmacrennan in Co Donegal was formed to subdue this trouble. Both of these armies met in battle at Kilmacrennan the result of which was a defeat for the native clans, this area was quiet but elsewhere in Ulster it was a different affair and resulted in Parliament sending General Munro and a Scottish army to Ulster where they landed at Carrickfergus in April 1642. The Church Elders in these regiments set up a Presbytery here on 10th June 1642, which was the first in Ulster. Derry was under siege, but this time success was not on their side and they had to withdraw.

At St Johnson the second Presbytery in Ulster was set up in 1654 as a result of the Carrickfergus regiment having been deployed there. In this year Urney Presbyterian Church was established but had no building. The First minister was Rev James Wallace who had been in the area for a short time before, taking services in the open and travelling to people's homes when needed. In 1655 he went with Jeremiah O' Quinn on horseback to Connaught on a mission. As both these men spoke fluent Irish they were able to speak to the people in their own language and be understood. In 1657 during his ministry he had to become a Commonwealth minister in the old Church of Ireland in Urney for a time. Bishops had absolute power in religious matters and Presbyterians were required to pay tithes to the established church and support their own minister as well. They were not allowed to vote, nor hold Government Office, and their marriages and baptisms could only be lawfully performed by the rector. His ministry lasted over twenty years.

The Second minister was Rev David Brown who came from Stirling in Scotland and ordained on 11 April 1677. Plans were drawn up for Urney's first church and in September 1680 records show that the building was completed. On 12 March 1689 King James had landed at Kinsale in Ireland and the scene was set for the siege of Derry. Rev Brown in common with all Protestants headed for safety in Derry, but died there in 1688 after eleven years service to his flock.

The third minister was Rev William Holmes who came on 22nd December.1696 his salary was £30.00 per year plus thirty barrels of corn and help with his crops when needed. In March 1700 seating arrangements caused friction as seats were of stool type and had no permanent position unlike the benches of today. Peace was restored and the Rev Holmes passed to eternal rest on 1734. It was during his ministry that a new Church Building was erected at Peacock Bank several miles away in 1734. it being thought that the Tullymoan building was needing repairs and was not very central in the parish and probably too small. The Rev Holmes died in October 1734 after nearly thirty-nine years of faithful ministry.

The Fourth minister was Rev William McBeath and was ordained on December 22nd 1737 and this was a short ministry because he transferred to Ushers Quay in Dublin in June 1745 where he remained until his death in 1755. On the third October 1740 a new site was being sought as a deed was signed on this date to purchase land almost halfway between the first and second church. Building started in 1745 and finished in 1749 and was constructed from locally quarried stone and had a thatch roof.

Urney Presbyterian Church. c1912

The Fifth minister was Rev Andrew Alexander who was ordained on 31st August 1749. He was to receive £50.00 per year and help with his crops at Gallony, near Inchaney. His ministry lasted fifty-nine years and he died on 30th April 1808 and reposes amongst his congregation in the old graveyard in Urney. He wrought long in the Lords vineyard and was a true and faithful servant. The Rev John Gillespie was the sixth minister who was ordained on 26th Jan. 1809. This was a difficult time with poor crops and severe weather. This ministry ended after 14 years with his death on 28th July 1823. The seventh minister was Rev James Purss ordained on 20th May 1824 and remained until his death on 29th August 1836. His mortal remains were interred in the old graveyard in Urney.

The Eighth minister was Rev John Mc Conagthy who was ordained on 14th June 1837. In 1838 massive repairs cost £184.50. In March 1845 the roof was replaced with bangor slates. This minister understood the value of education and it was through him that stables and session house with master's apartments were built and completed for the sum of £52.12. At this time he recorded the names of 674 individuals who belonged to his church, a drop from 950 in 1843 mostly due to famine and emigration. This hard working minister retired due to ill health in 1881 after an amazing fruitful ministry of forty-six years.

The Ninth minister was the Rev Matthew Neill who came from Devock, Co Antrim and was installed on 20th August 1881. Extensive repairs and alterations were carried out during this ministry. A new school beside the church was opened in 1906 to replace the old school with another at Tullywhisker in April 1910. On 18th April 1918 an organ was purchased for the first time. Prior to this a precentor led the congregation in the singing. Repairs were carried out by Olpherts of Castlefin in 1921. Rev Matthew Neill retired after 45 years of faithful service and died in 1926 and slumbers in his native soil in Dervock.

The Tenth minister was Rev John Thompson Montgomery who was installed on 11th Feb 1927 and came from Belfast. This was a shorter ministry, but during it a new heating furnace was installed costing £250.00 in 1936 and replaced the underground stoves from an earlier date. He was called home on 3rd October 1938 aged 61 years.

Urney School, built 1906, now the Church hall

The Eleventh minister was the Rev Kenneth Gregg who was ordained on 3rd March 1939. During the war he served as chaplain to the forces. Electricity was installed in 1953 ending the oil lamp era. A new wall surrounding the property was built in 1948. Rev Kenneth Gregg remained until 1964 when he took up another position after 25 years service. The Twelfth minister was Rev Ross Cahill who was installed on 7th January 1967 and during his time a new manse in Sion Mills was built at a cost of £8250 in 1969. A member of the congregation Mr Eric McKimmon became a minister on 27th June 1982. Rev Cahill retired on 24th June 1984. And was summoned home by his master on 3rd May 1986 and rests in his native Ballymena.

The Thirteenth minister was Rev David Edgar who was ordained on 13th March 1986 and came from Portadown. This was a very short ministry as he left in May 1990 to become chaplain in the Royal Airforce. The Fourteenth minister was Rev Robert Sterling who was installed on 3rd May 1991. During this time the 1906 school was adapted for a church hall as it had closed due to low numbers and this work cost £16,385.99.

During May 2001 Rev Sterling accepted a call to Clonlig, near Bangor after ten years ministry to us. The Fifteenth minister was Rev Trevor Williamson from Garvagh. He was installed on 6th September 2002 and during this time we coped with dry rot, extended the car park and purchased a new organ. During May 2010 he retired and this congregation now awaits his successor.

A speech By Rev. James Purss, Presbyterian minister of Urney, on 2nd May 1830 at a public dinner in Strabane in aid of funds for the newly erected Catholic Church.

"I Trust" said the Rev. Mr Purss, "that however I may dissent from some of my friends in certain speculative points of doctrine, they will do me the justice to admit, that I heartily coalesce with them in the grand essential which should ever designate the character of an honest member of society – I love my country and I love my kind. While I pursue my own opinions, I leave every man to the free enjoyment of his, for God alone, who ready the heart, can render acceptable the offerings of all. The several forms of religious worship, instead of affording subject for dispute, should serve as a stimulant for our greater zeal in his service, and I regard every form as sacred which is the spontaneous offering of the unfretted mind. I rejoice from my heart that those prejudices are progressively wearing away, which was founded in misconception of each other and too long fostered by the enemies of Ireland's peace. The enlightened of all parties have long sighed for the period when Irishmen of every denomination in possession of their civil and religious rights could turn their individual attentions to the happiness and prosperity of their common country, in which, as all are equally interested, all should equally share"

Farming, from tenant to Landlord
By Daniel Mc Menamin

Farming was a major part of the life of our ancestors in the Urney area going back many thousands of years. The land in Urney along the River Finn was some of the best in the area. Some of this would probably have been under the control of the Erenagh of Urney, O Ceallaigh/ O'Kelly. At the time of the plantation this land was confiscated from the Irish farmers and leased to farmers mostly of Scottish and English origin. Some of the farmers associated with the Tyrone side of Urney would have been included in the hearth money roll of 1666. John Crawford of Lower Urney, John Spear and Thomas Clarke of Inchenny, Edmond O'Doherty of Inisclan just some of the names still tending Urney farms in recent years. Connolly Gage's map of Urney west of 1816 tells us the names of farmers on the Donegal side around that time. H. and P. Mc Anulty of Drumconnell, Francis Mc Kinney of Graffy, Joseph Mc Cormick of Drumbane and Wm. Martin of Drumdoit, again names associated with farming in recent years.

The small villages around Urney, many called after the townland in which they were situated, would have been home to many farmers, labourer, cottiers and their families. These villages or 'clachan's' as they were called made up the nucleus of the settlement of the townland with very little one-off houses before 1800. Only the farmer would have lived in a farmhouse, the rest lived in small cottages which were then known as 'cabins', generally consisting of one room and a door to let in light and let out smoke. The census of 1841 showed that 40% of the population of Ireland lived in such conditions. Many of these 'cabins' would have been cold and damp. The Rev. James Jones, Rector of Urney wrote about cabins in Urney in 1836 "They are very poor cabins often run up without lime......They have bedsteads just sufficient to raise the bedding from the floor; the poor man lies upon straw or chaff, he has no sheets, and frequently not sufficient blankets; many people lie on the same bed". Many of the cottages not only housed the poor, but also their animals. These cabins known as "byre dwellings" had their benefits, the heat from the animals helped keep the family warm and the manure could be collected for use on their plot of land. The manure was simply thrown outside the cabin door. However Theobald Jones, Esq. of Urney house had this to say about that practice, "the greatest evil is the close neighbourhood, nay contact, of the manure heap to the house".

The cottiers system of farming is believed to have been a response to unemployment and lack of a fully developed money economy. The tenant farmer let the land from the landlord who in turn sub-let small plots of land to the cottier. Theobald Jones, explained how the cottier system worked in the Urney parish, "The cottier take is various; a house with a small garden, a cow's grass, one rood of flax land, two roods for oats and liberty to cut one day's cutting of turf, may be had for £7; a cabin and cows grass for £4 15s; a cabin without land from £1 to £1 10s." He further states that no money changes hands, the rent being "frequently paid for by Labour".

Leases for the land around Urney were signed between the landlord and the farmer with the following leases found for the Gage's land in Donegal.

- 8 Sept 1780. Lease to Mary, Nail and John O'Bogan Dunnaloob, Co D'gl. Lease of half townland of Dunnaloob for term of 31 years of yearly rent of £7 plus fees and duties.

- 10 Nov 1795 to Wm. Leitch Skelpy, Co D'gl. Counterpart lease of 65 acres, 28 perches of land in Skelpy for the term of lives of Ld. Visct. Hamilton, Hon. Claudius Hamilton, and Johnston Mansfield, eldest son of Robt. Mansfield of Killygordan on term of 31 years at yearly rent of £15.9s.0p

- 24 April 1798. To Henry O' Neil Claudy, Co Tyrone. Lease of part of townland of Dresnagh for term of 14 years at yearly rent of £9.3s.9p plus duties.

- 15 Nov 1814. To Charles Lafferty Gortkilly, farmer. Lease of 4 acres 2 roods 14 perches, lands in Drumconnell Co Donegal, for the term of life of Sir. Jas. Galbraith, Urney, Co Donegal or 20 years of a yearly rent of £8 10s 8d. and covenant to plant 10 forest trees each year, plus duties 8 hens.

- 15 Nov 1814. To Francis, Hugh (junr) and Felix Mc Kinney, all of Tullyard, Co Donegal weavers. Lease of 28 acres 1 rood 26 perches for life of Sir Jas. Galbraith Urney Co Donegal or 20 years at rent of £13. 13s 0d and covenant to plant 13 forest trees each year plus duties 3 hens.

Frank and John Mc Kinney, Tullyard 1936

John Mc Evoy in his Statistical Survey of Tyrone (1802) states "I believe there is no better potatoe and flax farmers in the kingdom, than those of Tyrone", and James McParlan in his statistical survey of Donegal (1801) reports "Along the fin-water, is quite a tillage and manufacturing country, beside an abundance of potatoes, oats, and barley; flax is grown here and manufactured to a very considerable extent". Potatoes were normally planted by the "Irish or lazy-bed" method especially on higher ground; this proved to be a highly effective way of reclaiming unfertile land. Despite having the better ground not everything went well for the farmers on the lower ground, An Abercorn letter dated 11-10-1751 reported that "Floods carry away corn and hay on the rivers Finn and Mourne". Almost all farms had at least one pig fed on potatoes which was fattened and sold to pay for any bills that may arise. Pigs were known as "the gentleman who pays the rent".

The Great Famine of 1845-47 was to have a devastating effect on the poor farmer. After the famine the cottier farmer and the smaller tenant farmer practically disappeared through starvation and emigration. The villages and the cabins in which they lived were mostly left derelict and the cottiers that were left stayed on as labourers for a day's wage. This had the effect of making the farms in the area bigger with the amalgamation of several smaller farms.

Discontent following the famine led to the Tenant Right League of the 1850s and the Land League of 1879. The government was forced to introduce several land acts; the most successful act was the Wyndham act of 1903. This act allowed tenants to buy out the landlord at favourable rates and by 1921 75% of tenant farmers had bought their own holdings. For many this was the first time the tenant farmers truly owned their own land, a lord over their own 'small' Estate.

URNEY 1856. Families chiefly employed in	
Agriculture	644
Manufacture, trade, mills	120
Other	167

LAND SOLD IN URNEY

10 June 1749.
"Know all men by these presents that whereas I Oliver Mc Casland of Strabane in the County of Tyrone Esq. have granted bargained and sold my forth part or share as now divided of the Ls Ship of manor of Castlefinn in the County of Donegal to Conolly Mc Causland of Fruithill in the County of Lderry And Hodson gage of Ballymargy."

8 Feb 1752. "Hodgson Gage, and Conolly Mc Cauisland, agreement that Hodgson Gage will pay bond of £1,035 remaining sum due for purchase of manor of Castlefinn."

7th June 1840. Theophilus Jones to Alexander Turner – land at Kennystown.

4th April 1841. Theophilus Jones to Moses Chambers – land at Glentown.

21st February 1862. James Hamilton to James Thompson – land at Kennystown.

LAND FOR SALE IN URNEY

11th sept 1865. "To be sold that portion of the lands of Urney, as now in the possession of the owner, Thomas John Knox, Esq. and his under tenants. These lands are situated in the best part of County Tyrone, within three miles of Strabane, a Market Town and Station on the Irish North-Western line of Railway, and within fifteen miles of Londonderry. They are in a high state of cultivation, and are set to a prosperous and industrious tenantry and comprise about 1,030 acres of arable and pasture Land, yielding a well paid profit- rent of £547 12s 6d. The property is capable of considerable improvement, and by a judicious outlay, the rental could be considerably increased."

LAND TO LET IN URNEY

5th April 1825

The farm called Cressy, near Claudy Bridge, containing 54 acres, all at present under stock; an excellent house and offices on the farm. Also, a farm in Urney, between the Church and Claudy, containing about 30 acres of choice land, all in high condition, laid down with Clover and grass Seed. Mr. Ash at Urney Park, will shew the Premises; and for terms apply to Mr M. M'Laughlin, Castlefin.

TO BE LET

THE MILL and Farm of MAGHERACALLAGHAN, containing Twenty-two Acres of Land, for the term of Two Lives, and the remainder of a Lease of Thirty-One Years. Security will be required at the commencement of said term. Proposals will be received by SAMUEL BROWN, Esq. who adjoins the premises. July 27, 1812.

The old mill at Magherycallaghan, built in 1834

Urney Chocolates, Sweet Success

By William Haire

As the First World War drew to a close Henry T. Gallagher (Harry), his wife Eileen (nee Cullen) and their three children moved from Co. Donegal to a new home in Urney, Co. Tyrone, almost a mile from Clady on the road to Strabane. An old three storey Rectory that had a mature garden and orchard and extensive grounds had come on the market and this was deemed suitable for the family needs. At the time Harry was the Crown Solicitor for Co. Donegal and the new home wasn't that much further from his employment.

Mrs. Gallagher was soon tending her family in their new home and became aware of the flowers and fruit trees in abundance in their gardens. It was obvious to her that there was more than they would need for their own use and so her mind soon turned to finding ways to make some good use of the surplus. Around this time there was very little work locally and as a result many of the local girls left for the far off shores of America or England in an effort to improve their lot. Mrs. Gallagher was determined to help a few of these girls, at least, to find some work locally. It is known that she shipped early season flowers, including snowdrops and violets from her gardens to Covent Garden market in London. This was quite easy at the time as there were rail and shipping services available then which enabled the flowers to arrive in good fresh condition, which meant they commanded a good price.

Any surplus fruit was bottled or made into jam and found a ready market locally. The business continued to expand but a major problem arose when the need for sugar exceeded the amount that was available under the rationing system in place at the time. Further supplies of sugar were refused but they were informed that they might be able to get sugar for the manufacture of sweets. Harry and Eileen duly went to Dublin to plead their case with the Controller of Sugar. There they met Mr. Rodney O'Donnell, a Derry man, who again explained that because of the scarcity and rationing of sugar he couldn't give them any for jam making, but he could give them sugar for the making of sweets. The only option left for the Gallagher's was to learn how to make sweets.

At the first opportunity experiments in sweet making began on the kitchen stove. After a few failures it was found that Fudge and Raspberry Cream topped the success list. The new business began to take shape in the basement of their home. Other flavours were soon added to the list and different ingredients were experimented with and recipes adjusted in an attempt to expand the range. Mrs. Gallagher was the sole salesperson as well as the manufacturer of the range of sweets initially. One customer soon followed up his initial order with another larger one and after a comment on how quickly they sold and enquiry as to how his customers liked the sweets, she was advised "The Farmers find them great in their tea as the sugar is still rationed."

It wasn't long before a man was employed full time to deliver the sweets to local shops over an ever-expanding area. During a visit to a Trade Fair in Scotland, Mrs. Gallagher met an old school friend who was engaged in a similar business and after an extended conversation, the idea of making chocolate was planted in her mind. By 1921 the Urney boxed range of "Nora Assortment" was launched. It may be noted that although they were good employers the Gallaghers were not to be cheated, in 1921, at Strabane Quarter Sessions, Urney Chocolate Factory sued two former employees for eight shillings (40 pence in today's money): the value of caps and aprons they took with them when they left their employment. A decree was granted for the full amount.

A chocolate mould found along the river Finn.

In 1921 the first major disaster struck Urney Chocolates when a serious fire left the basement and house an empty shell. A temporary wooden bungalow was quickly built in the grounds as a new home, Harry then proceeded to build a new purpose built chocolate factory for Eileen a short distance from their former home. It gave them much more room and it had the most up-to-date machinery for chocolate and sweet manufacture installed. It was operational in less than a year after the disastrous fire.

On Friday, January 6, 1922 at Urney the Gallagher family held a dance in their new factory for the workers and guests, 300 people attended. DAN MOLLOY'S orchestra rendered the music for the dancing and local artists contributed songs and recitations. The evening's entertainment was conducted by MR. HEALEY (excise officer Strabane) and MR. NEWTOWN, (manager). A sumptuous supper was served at midnight and an abundant choice of chocolates was sent around a number times. The factory had been tastefully and artistically decorated and all were full of gratitude to the promoters for providing such a pleasant and successful event. On the afternoon of Friday THE FEAST OF THE EPIPHANY it was the children of Clady and district who were treated. There was a large sized Christmas tree and a musical programme concluding with an excellent tea and the children appreciated to the utmost these lovely treats and kindness they received.

A new range of chocolates "Maeve", was announced which were better and more delicious than before. These were sold in boxes at 3/6 per pound, 17½ pence in today's money, or loose if you desired. A photograph of the period shows around fifty employees, mainly girls. Everything seemed to be going well until the afternoon of February 12th 1924, when just after the workers had taken their noon break, a worker in the area spotted flames and raised the alarm. Despite everyone's efforts, the new factory was totally destroyed. All that remained of it were the scorched walls as a photo taken at the time shows. It would appear that a mixture of boiling sugar and chocolate, a very volatile mixture, left simmering until after the lunch break had boiled over and caught fire from the heat source used.

The workers didn't need to be told of their impending unemployment when they returned from lunch and one can only guess how the Gallagher's felt on seeing their recent £20,000 investment now lying in ruins. Undaunted by this recent loss, Harry and Eileen were considering rebuilding again when the recently established Free State Government raised a duty of 6d (2 ½ pence) per lb on chocolate imports. As the majority of their sales were in the South, this levy would make their products more expensive and as Harry no longer had his job as State Solicitor for back-up, moving south looked a more attractive option to pursue.

They looked at various options and were eventually shown the old airfield in Tallaght. It looked promising but they encountered many difficulties in their efforts to raise the necessary finance. They were even considering moving to Canada when the finances they sought were put in place allowing them to proceed with their next bold adventure. They set up the new factory on a shoestring at Tallaght. As money had to be conserved initially, they had no refrigeration plant to cool the chocolate in the moulds or to keep the milk cool. Harry overcame this problem by having the factory work at night when the chocolate and sweets were able to cool naturally. This meant that for a time Harry worked in the factory by night and in the office by day, so sleep was a rarity for him. A number of people who had previously worked at Urney moved to the new factory at Tallaght. One such worker was Willie McElwee, from Gallony, who ended up as the manager of the Enrobing Department and had family connections with Urney and its successors until closure.

Workers at Urney Chocolate Factory the day after it was burned to the ground

In 1926, the company was granted a loan of £11,000 under the 1924 Trade Loans Act to further their expansion. When Harry advertised six new posts available, three hundred people turned up for interview such was the demand for jobs at that time. Not long into 1927, the fledging company was troubled by rumours that cross-channel interests who were not Irishmen controlled them. This caused great concern because it affected their sales. On 30th April 1927, the company advertised a reward of £100 for information, which would lead to the source of these mischievous rumours and to further clarify matters they stated that the company directors were Harry and Eileen Gallagher and Tim and Nora Callanan.

In 1927, "TARA" boxed chocolates were now available at 4 shillings (20 pence) per pound and in 1930 "GENERAL DELIGHT" Five division bars cost 2d each. In 1928, GILBERT GALBRAITH, a reporter visited the factory at Tallaght and found great pride amongst the workforce who had by now excellent facilities not found in factories locally. These included recreation grounds for games and pastimes, luncheon rooms and recreation halls for concerts, debates and dramatic performances. A reading room and excellent library offered ready facilities for intellectual recreation and self-education, sure to produce a more valuable sense of citizenship with understanding and vision for all possibilities for social betterment. By 1940, a trickle of exports to Britain had begun and after this world sales began to develop. Urney was only a small company compared to its competitors but the quality of their products so impressed Lowney's of Canada that they issued a licence for Urney to manufacture chocolates on their behalf to be sent to Canada. Soon after another North American firm placed a contract with Urney to manufacture "CHARMS" for the European and other markets.

Expansion

Urney bought the English confectionery firm of B.C. Murch and soon removed the machinery to Tallaght where they began to manufacture the Murch product range. These were then shipped to England where the team of ten salesmen, formerly employed by B.C. Murch, simply carried on as before. In 1962 Schrafft's of America signed a contract with Urney to manufacture chocolate bars for them for sale in America despite fierce competition from their competitors. Mr. C.D Kelly, General Sales Manager of Urney, signed the contract in Boston. A consignment of 1,000,000 bars left Dublin on 24th August and was the first of their regular fortnightly deliveries.

In 1962 Urney also opened a new £100,000 plant for the manufacture of "Urney Big Bars". An Taoiseach, Mr. Sean Lemass, who praised the way Urney were meeting the challenge of the Common Market, officially opened the new plant. The new ranges were a different shape and size from previous bars and included "Regal Milk, Milk Tray, Nut Cream and Turkish Delight". Newspapers, television and radio announced this new venture to the public and the phrase "Any time is Urney time" was coined. Exports from Urney accounted for over £1,000,000.

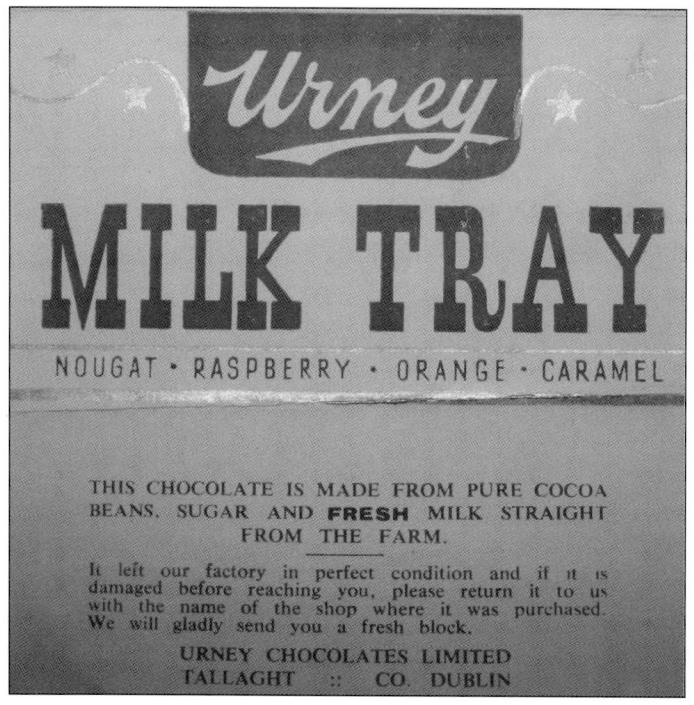

Urney Wrapper

In November 1962, Urney Chocolates South Africa (Proprietary) Ltd., a subsidiary of the Tallaght firm, bought over the South African firm of Chapelat Industries, which had been formed fifty years earlier. The share value was £500,000 in 5/=(25p) shares and £65,000 in 6% preference shares. Chapelat Industries comprised of four factories, two in Johannesburg and two in Capetown, which had combined sales of over £2,000,000 and a workforce of 1,100 in their Garden Factory. In 1965 it employed 850 people and exported more than £1 ½ million worth of goods. Its largest markets were in the U.S., Canada and Britain, but considerable quantities went to the Far East, Malta, Gibraltar, Australia, Norway and Sweden. Their recent link-up with the Dutch company of Van Houtens added several hundreds of thousands of pounds to export sales.

When Harry retired his son Redmond took over at the helm of this empire. Redmond was a keen motor sport enthusiast and won prizes in his car "The Leprechaun." Redmond was prevailed upon to give up his passion and settle instead for the thrill of running the business. In 1963 W.R.Grace, an Irish American who already owned HB Dairies bought over the remaining shares of Urney Chocolates and applied strict budgetary controls with little investment being made in the business. The name Urney Chocolates was changed to HB Chocolates in 1970. The parent company soon found that trading conditions in America were becoming less profitable and set about the sale of its Irish assets. They tried to dispose of their two Irish businesses, the former Urney and HB dairies, for some time before an offer by Unilever was accepted in 1973.Even after they introduced a new product, "The Catch Bar" successfully it was a struggle to survive in the market conditions prevailing. The final straw came when the E.E.C. abolished subsidies on butter and chocolate in 1979. The HB Chocolate, formerly Urney Chocolate factory closed for good in 1980.

The name Urney Chocolates has not been used since the former factory became a DIY store in 1980, until recently. An enterprising manufacturer L.C. Confectionery, Co Kildare bought up several of the product names of the past and already the public can enjoy Cleeves Toffee Bars and Jedward Easter Eggs, which are produced by them, trading as Urney Chocolates. Further chocolate delights await the customer during the incoming year of 2010/2011. JEDWARD are the popular teenage identical twins who appeared on X-factor in 2009.

The interior of the burned out Chocolate Factory

Flax Mills

By Mary Mc Corkell

The cool damp climate and soil type in the locality of Urney and surrounding areas suited the growing of flax very well. In the late nineteenth century and up to mid twentieth local farmers and labourers who rented small areas of land from them grew flax for the eventual production of linen fabric for which Ireland is famous. The industry was at its peak during the war years with many farmers taking advantage of British government grants to increase the production of flax. The seed was planted in early spring on well prepared soil and by mid summer produced small pale blue flowers. When the flowers died and brown seed heads formed late August/ early September on three feet high stalks it was ready for harvesting. This is when the really hard work began and involved many local men, some women and older boys and girls. Work was scarce and the economic climate so different from what we have today that people were glad of the work even if the wages were small. The flax plant is very tough, with long thin fibres that run along the full length of the stalk just under an outer straw like covering and in the centre of the plant is a woody core. A sticky substance called pectin holds the plant parts together.

Pulling Flax (Lint)
The plant was pulled root and all in handfuls to get the full length of the fibres rather than cutting which would have wasted too much of the valuable flax nearest the root. This was labour intensive back breaking work from eight in the morning to six or later. My brother remembers helping our Uncle Jimmy Clarke pull lint for John O Flaherty after school. He admired his organized method and easy relaxed movement along the field grabbing large handfuls of lint and dropping them on the ground as he went along. Paddy Mc Gee said a "heavy crop was pulled by the acre and a light crop by the stook". It took 12 beets to make a stook. This was how workers were paid, not by the hour so it was in their interest to pull as much as possible in order to earn as much as they could. A worker was paid about 2 shillings (10p) a stook . This was probably the reason women and children in the family helped out. Some of the young ones were paid a few shillings and some weren't. Four good workers could pull an acre a day.

As a boy Paddy used to carry tea and scone bread to one of the workers in the field. The tea was in a tin can or a bottle corked with rolled newspaper. He said the man he carried it to would pour the tea out in disgust whenever his sister sweetened it with saccharin instead of sugar which was probably rationed at the time. Of course some choice expletives were aired in the act. His pay on a Saturday was two shillings and sixpence, the going rate for these young people. Joe Hunter said he managed to pull a rood of flax in a day, good going for a young lad. The workers tied the pulled lint into bundles called beets as they went along. These beets were left standing roots upwards in the field neatly against each other in stooks ready for the next stage of retting. The bands that held the beets together were made from rushes. Cecil Darragh whose father owned a scutch mill in Glentown (Killen's mill, David Killen was his grandfather) told me that he used to go to neighbouring fields belonging to Maggie Connolly or Walter Mc Grath to gather rushes to make bands in preparation for lint pulling time. At home he and his brothers made the bands by twisting six or more long rushes together to make them strong enough to hold the beets together. They were made in such a way that they could expand when the beets swelled up with water without breaking and then tightened in again when they dried out. They made up hundreds at a time and hung them over a rope. John O Flaherty had more permanent ties or bands made out of straw into ropes which were used every year. School boys were employed to gather up these bands when they were finished with them at the end of the season to be used the following season.

Workers and children posing for photographs at Hamilton's mill Clady

Retting

A hole twenty by thirty yards was dug out near a burn or a stream. This was in a low lying area of the farm. Water flowed from higher ground into the hole. It was plugged at the bottom end with a sod which stemmed the flow of water from the other end until the right amount of water entered. This was known as a lint dam which held three to four feet of water. The water was stagnant and had a scum on top which got thicker with algae as time passed. The beets were taken by horse and cart to the lint dam when ready to be soaked or retted. Placing them in the dam in the correct order was important, tight together side by side in rows roots downwards in a single layer but not touching the bottom, until the dam was full. This was usually done manually to prevent damage to the flax. Then more water was added to almost cover the beets. Tramping to hold them in the water was often done by girls and women until weighted down by large stones keeping them just under the water for ten to fourteen days. Tramping every now and then on top of the stones ensured the beets stayed under the water. The retting time depended on the type of water and the weather.

The purpose of soaking the lint was to break down the sticky pectin that held the plant components together. It had to ferment in the water and in the process gave off a terrible stench that permeated the area which everyone I talked to vividly remembers. Knowing when to remove the beets from the dam required the expertise of the farmer or somebody else who had the feel for this process. Cecil Darragh said they got Mickey Lafferty to test when their lint was ready. He would take a few stalks out of the water and rub it between his fingers and if the fibre separated easily from the stem it was ready for drying. It was just as important not to over steep them.

Removing the beets from the dam

This was a difficult task, cold, dirty and very smelly. Beets heavy with water had to be manually lifted out to prevent damage to the fibres. Workers, wearing long rubber aprons and boots stood in the dam knee deep in water while doing this. The smell of the putrid water clung to their clothes and skin for days even after washing. I was told that some farmers unplugged the dam letting some of the water out before removing beets. This sounded sensible and less dirty than standing in the stinking cold water. They were left to drain on the bank at the side of the dam for several hours. They were then loaded on to a cart for transport to the field for drying.

There were four lint dams in the field in front of the old mill in Clady where the Smuggler's car park is now. Nine or ten were in a field on the Tullymoan road. Many more were dotted around the countryside near the flax fields. David Darragh said his father had an agreement with J O'Flaherty to hold water in their storage dam for twenty four hours at a time. One very dry season J O'Flaherty who had water rights asked them for use of this water for his lint dam. He was given the key (handle) that opened the sluice gate to release some of the water.

Grassing or drying the flax.
Beets were dropped off the cart at intervals, untied and the lint spread thinly and evenly in rows in a field of short grass to dry out in the wind and sun, a process referred to as "grassing." This airing continued the loosening of the fibres from the other parts of the stalk. As the workers spread the contents of each beet in the field the same ties or bands that secured them were dropped beside them on the ground. These would be used again to tie the beets together when dried. Weather dictated the drying time which was usually one or two weeks.

Lifting
The dried lint was lifted with a tool made from the flat handle of a galvanized bucket. The curved shape of the handle made the task easier. It had a grip at one end and was sharp at the other. Women and children helped the men do this job. The original bands were used to tie the dried beets again for transporting to the mill. Nancy Mc Gee helped to gather the lint in her father's field in Ballybun. It was ready for scutching at this stage. This happened when other farm work could be put off or when weather dictated it. Until the scutcher was ready the beets were stored in stacks and placed on top of stones or twigs just slightly off the damp ground to keep them dry. If they were to be kept for a longer period they were thatched over with rushes and tied down with grass ropes until ready to be taken to the scutch mill. The field where they were stored was called a stack garden.

Farmers brought the beets of lint to the mill on a cart when they wanted it scutched. Each was marked, dated and weighed carefully on arrival as flax varied greatly in quality according to how well it was grown and harvested. In O'Flaherty's mill in Clady this was one of Frank Mc Gee's many jobs. He was the farm manager and had responsibility for overseeing not only scutching work and all that it entailed but also making up the books and workers' wages at the end of the week. His son Cyril recalls how they daren't make a sound in the house when his father did the accounts every weekend.

"Mc Gees on a Friday Night

*On a Friday night we were quiet as mice
As the ready reckoner came out
For O'Flaherty's men
Dad took up the pen
Their wages for to account
A glowering look was all it took
To cease our chattering voices
For us twas no fun, but when he was done
The wireless gave other choices."*

Stacks of dried flax ready for scotching

Scutching

Scutching got rid of the central woody core and the outer straw covering to release the precious fibres from the flax stalk. This was very complicated and by far the most dangerous job in the mill and involved more skill than before. This was usually done in one building which had a loft to store the flax. John O Flaherty's mill in Clady was quite up market at the time having two buildings to do the scutching. These were in operation since the early 1940's. All the scutching work used to be carried out in the **old** mill situated over the chapel road. There are two houses on that site today. The **new** mill was at the bottom of the street where the Smugglers restaurant is now. This was formerly used as a dairy and older Clady people still refer to it as such before becoming the roller mill and the finished scutching was done in the old mill. Mills were sited near streams to make use of the water to provide power for the waterwheel. A weir blocked the water in the stream to build a good amount or head of water which was directed via a head race to a man made pond called a dam where it was stored until needed to drive the waterwheel. A sluice gate released a rush of water along the mill race to strike the wheel making it turn and start the mill machinery. When there wasn't sufficient water to drive the wheel scutching was interrupted or an oil engine had to be used instead.

Roller Mill

In the new mill the dried flax was processed for scutching by breaking and loosening the unwanted straw like covering and woody core. There were special rollers in this mill for the job. They consisted of a series of cogged wheels with deep grooves that turned against each other to crush and mangle the flax. There wasn't a wheel to drive this mill. Nelie Nelis remembers a tractor situated behind the mill that generated the power to drive the rollers. Steam was another source of power produced by fires of shows behind the mill. Mrs O'Flaherty said that her husband paid £3,000 to have electricity installed in the mills about mid 1940's and shortly after this the village houses and other businesses benefited.

Four men worked at the rollers in the new mill assembly line style. First worker, a **stricker** opened the beets and placed the flax on the platform (*3ft wide*) in front of the roller. His pay was £2 a week. Second worker was a **shaker out**. He shook the flax to loosen it. Third worker the **roller man** fed it through the rollers and was paid £3 a week.

Fourth worker, locally known as a **twister** took it off the rollers, twisted it under his arm and put it on a cage ready for the proper scutching. This looked like an upturned table. It wasn't unusual for young boys or women get the flax ready for rolling, as described in the first and second stages. I was told by a neighbour that her sixteen year old sister worked in the roller mill for nine weeks. She replaced her brother who became ill at the time and rather than lose the work and wages for the family she was sent to cover for him.

The mill owner was reluctant to employ her but she was up to the job so he kept her on. The waste material that fell off the rollers called **shows** was of no use to the farmer who brought the lint or to the miller but was of great value to the villagers who burned it as fuel for heating and cooking. Cecil Darragh recalled coming to the mill in Clady for shows to bed chickens after his father's mill ceased to operate. It was one man's job to take shows from the mill for storage in a "lean to" next to the mill and they were available free of charge for anyone who wanted them.

Poor quality lint could be used to thatch barns or as bedding for animals. Nothing went to waste. The seed heads could be fed to chickens. My brother said he saw workers feeding seeds to small birds like linnets and goldfinches. The **tow** often known as the rug which had short fibres and looked like sheeps wool was graped on to a cart and taken to the far scutch mill. **Targers** scutched the tow leaving it white and soft and still very dusty. It was packed into bales sewn up with binder twine and weighed. This was sold separately at the market as it was of inferior quality. Strangely enough the farmer received no money for the tow. The mill owner claimed it and sold it at the market.

Scutching

The old mill as it was known by was where the highly skilled and dangerous finishing of the flax was done by scutchers who stood at berths where there were wiper blades or handles to do the scutching. The number of berths depended on the size of the mill. O' Flaherty's had eight. Darragh's had four and Hamilton's had six.

Taking a well earned rest 1. ??? 2. Hugh Clarke (centre),
3. Frank Nelis, 4. Joe Hamilton, 5. Charlie Hagan (front).

Back Row L-R 1. Margaret Mc Shea (O'Neill), 2. Eliz Mc Shea (Hamilton), 3. ???
4. Mrs Deveanny. 5. ???
Front Row L-R 1. ??? 2. Paddy Mc Goldrick, 3. Joe Hamilton 4. ??? 5.??? 6. Charlie Haughey.

The scutcher picked up a handful of flax, wrapped it around his hand and held it against a steel plate as a set of swiftly spinning wooden blades or handles as they were called beat off the remaining shows leaving long fine fibres. He turned the flax in his hand to clean the other end. Great care and attention were vital to prevent loss of a finger by the swiftly revolving blades. Joe Hunter said there was a sudden change in the noise of the machine from a whir to a whacking sound when a worker sustained an injury. Some scutchers worked in pairs one taking off the rough and the other perfecting the job. The first was a **buffer** and the one who finished the scutching a **cleaner.** The man who finished scutching the tow was called a **targer.** Scutchers moved from area to area to work in mills. Joe Hunter remembers a time when his father Johnny, Jimmy Nelis and my grandfather, Hugh Clarke walked from Clady to Donemana to work, leaving at 5am and getting home 7pm. They were paid two pounds six pence per stone of scutched flax and would have scutched 4 stone in a day

Finished scutched flax

The result was long strong shiny white fibres like hair. It was neatly wound and tied into hanks and dropped into a box or frame, then graded marked and weighed. It took 13 hanks to make a stone. Cecil Darragh said their flax was always a good grade. The farmer paid the miller who kept the tow in payment for scutching. The scutcher was paid for each good stone of flax and not for scutching the tow. There was no such thing as weights and measures regulation to safeguard the rights of the farmer so he had to take the millers word. The finished product was usually sold at Strabane market. Paddy Mc Ghee remembers a time when O "Flaherty's mills operated for a full year day and night because they scutched for many farmers. It had to be a good harvest that year. Good quality flax resulted in fine linen. Poor flax made tow hence a poorer quality cloth.

Some Irish scutched fibre was processed in Herdsman's Sion Mills. An employee who worked in the spinning department told me that out of the fourteen machines just one was used to process Irish flax. Most flax came from Belgium and some from Russia.

Working Conditions

Working conditions were a far cry from today's standards. They were primitive dangerous dirty noisy and cold if working late in the year. The dust in the mill was so thick it was difficult to see. It clung to the workers' clothes and faces particularly around their noses. Throats were dry and noses clogged with dust. They eagerly looked forward to their tea breaks.

One can imagine the state of their lungs after breathing the powdery dust for days from early morning to night. Scutchers got the name of being hardened drinkers whether they deserved it or not. A well known complaint locally was mill fever (not medically confirmed) and treated with a good helping of whisky or the like. This occurred usually after scutching was finished and payment settled up. The hazard of fire in the mill with the shows meant that there was no heating even in winter.

I haven't heard of any major accidents in this mill but there was a very serious one in Hamilton's mill in the centre of the village. One of the owners Bob Hamilton lost part of his leg as he was in the process of starting up an oil engine to power the machinery during a dry period. This was a cooperative mill prior to Hamilton's ownership. It was badly damaged in a fire as the following article from the Chronicle 3/2/2011states.

100 YEARS AGO/1911

Clady Mill gutted

TWO men have been charged after Clady Mill was gutted between the hours of 3am and 5am. The mill was the property of the Urney Flax Co-Operative Society and was gutted by fire.

How the outbreak orginated is not as yet known. The damage is estimated at £500.

The matter was reported to police and as a result a man from Clady and another from Sion Mills were arrested. At a special sitting of the Petty Sessions, they were charged with maliciously setting the mill alight. The prisoners were conveyed to Derry Jail.

The Waterwheel

To start the mill a sluice gate was opened by the miller to let a good surge of water from the dam flow to the waterwheel causing it to turn. There were different kinds of wheel depending upon where the water hit it. Patsy Mc Ginley said the waterwheel in Mc Daid's Ballylast was overshot, the water entering at the top and it turned in an anti clockwise direction. The water ran down from Croaghan hill and was regulated further down. O'Flaherty's was also overshot. The water hit the wheel in Darragh's mill half way up. This is called breastshot. If the water hit the wheel at the bottom it was known as undershot. The overshot wheel produced more energy than the other types.

The machinery in the mill was linked to the wheel by its axle. The wiper blades or handles were attached to a long shaft from the wheel outside the mill wall. As it turned speed gathered to drive the rollers and wiper blades. These spun so fast you couldn't see them and often resulted in injuries to hands and fingers.

This photograph of the remnants of a waterwheel between Cloughfin and Lifford is the only one that still stands in the area. The mill had long ceased to operate at the time. It once belonged to a German called Wagendrieber who married a lady from Lifford by the name of Clarke.

Waterwheel between Cloghfin and Lifford

Scutch mills in the area

Co Tyrone

O'Flaherty's,	Clady village
Hamilton's,	Clady village
(formerly a co-operative)	
Barr's,	Scotstown Road
Purdon's,	Glentown
Inch's,	Urney Road
Darragh's,	Glentown
(formerly Killen's grandfather of Darragh's)	

Co Donegal

Taylor's	Tamnacrum
Mc Cormack's	Magheracallaghan
Temple's	Cloghard
Dan Mc Daid's (junior)	Gortin South
Portsallagh	near Gortfad
Bradley's	Churchtown
Dan Mc Daid's	Ballylast
(once owned by Patterson Castlefinn)	

A POEM BY ROBERT BURNS, BALLYLAST, LIFFORD.

(Cira 1930)

The land I love is "Eirn's Isle", to it my heart does turn,
And my early friend's in Clady, on the banks of the river Finn,
For thirty long years a scutcher, there in the old scutch mills I did toil,
I never thought I'd bid adieu to my dear old native soil.

Oh the happy days that I spent there I often do recall,
With Haugheys, the Elliots, Clarkes and McDaids, they were scutchers one and all,
Who shared with me their merry coin, while the wipers round did go,
In the Grand Old Mills of Clady where the River Finn does flow.

Now when that Saturday night would come, in the Village we all would stay,
There to drink each others Health and while the time away,
By Bairds big roaring fire we assembled in a row,
To smoke and drink and tell old tales of days so long ago

Now to the scutch mills of Clady, I'll bid a fond Adieu
And all the scutchers there that dwell so loyal kind and true,
Here roaming in a foreign land my thoughts to you do turn,
Oh for one night with my old friends, On the Banks of the River Finn.

Urney - History / People / Place

The natives scenes and comrades true I never will see more,
Though many friends here visit me who come from Erin's shore,
I love to have a drink with them and talk the while they stay,
Of my native haunt, I'll never see more three thousand miles away.

An Irish Exile here I dwell, my hair as white as snow,
My lamp of life shall soon be burned where the Delaware does flow,
If I had one glimpse of my native land I never, more would mourn,
And in peace I here would close my eyes, far far from the Glentown Burn.

But as an exile here I stay, eighty-two years old,
so adieu dear friends a foreign grave my body soon will hold,
Put those Irish words above my tomb so brightly shall be shown,
Telling that I was born in Clady in the County of Tyrone.

Fair day

By Daniel mc Menamin

Fairs have been taking place in the Urney area for hundreds of years for the sale of livestock and farm produce. Castlefinn held several fairs throughout 1801, January 4th, April 19th, June 7th, August 9th, October 4th, and November 22nd being mentioned. Samuel Lewis Topographical dictionary of 1837 states for Clady "Fairs for the sale of cattle, sheep, and pigs, are held on Aug. 1st and November 16th". An ordnance survey memoir of Urney (1838) mentions four fairs held in Clady "an inconsiderable village situated on the river Finn". It goes on to say that two of these Fairs were transferred to Strabane with the other two being held on May 16th and November 16th, and Slater's directory of 1870 mentions that fairs were held in Clady on May 17th and November 7th. Some of the early fairs evolved in the early 1800's to the hiring of farm workers on a six month contract. Strabane hiring fairs were held over two days, 12th/ 13th May and 12th / 13th November and were known as 'the rabble'.

Strabane was packed on a fair day with all the stallholders setting up early to sell their wares or make a few bob entertaining the crowds singing and dancing. 'Old Kelly' and his fiddle would keep the crowd going with favourite songs like 'The Day Bella Brooks was Drowned' and 'Old Killeter Fair' with 'O Donnell' playing jigs and reels with his violin on the back street.

Strabane on a fair day in the 1920's

Many of the people coming to Strabane to be hired came from west Donegal and they came to 'the Lagan' with very little English. 'The Lagan' was anywhere east of the Finn and Lagan valleys. For many 'the Lagan' meant slavery, struggle, hard work and long hours. For others however they found a new home, and in a lot of cases settled down and got married.

Ellen McFadden left her native Gweedore to be hired in Letterkenny; however she had mistaken the dates and had to travel a further twenty miles to Strabane fair. Ellen was hired to a widow woman called Margaret Kelly. Mrs Kelly owned a farm outside Clady, and it was to this farm Ellen was hired. Ellen nursed Mrs Kelly for the last three years of her life and when Mrs Kelly's son died he left the farm to Ellen.

The Donegal writer Patrick MacGill on being hired on a farm in Tyrone aged 14 wrote "In the morning I was called at 5 o' clock and sent out to wash potatoes in a stream near the house. Afterwards they were boiled in a pot over the kitchen fire, and when cooked they were eaten by the pigs and me. I must say that I was allowed to pick the best potatoes for myself, and I got a bowl of buttermilk to wash them down. The pigs got buttermilk also. That was my breakfast for the six months. For the dinner I got potatoes and buttermilk, for supper buttermilk and potatoes. I never got tea in the afternoon. The Bennets (his employers) took tea themselves, but I suppose they thought that such a luxury was unnecessary for me"

The fairs were often a rowdy and disorderly affair with 'the Urney mob' causing trouble at a fair in 1814. The ordnance survey memoir of Urney reported in 1838 "The fairs seem to benefit no portion of the community but keepers of public houses and are a source of quarrels and disorderly conduct on the part of those who frequent them"

The hiring fairs started to die out from the 1920's when workers began to move away from hiring fairs to the newly emerging factories in Britain, the school attendance act of 1926 (Free State) kept the younger Donegal workers at school longer and the increasing use of machinery meant intensive labour was no longer required. The last hiring in Strabane is believed to have taken place around 1949.

The Grand River Finn

By Daniel Mc Menamin

The river Finn (Abhainn na Finne), a slow steady river winding its way through the 'Vale of Urney'. The river and its source, Lough Finn is believed to have been named after Finngheal who drowned in the Lough while trying to save her brother Feardhomhain from a wild boar. The story goes when Feardhomhain was on his way home one day after a long journey he got into a fight with a wild boar. The wild boar was getting the better of Feardhomhain so he roared out for help. Finngheal on hearing the cries of her brother across the lake tied up her long hair, grabbed her sword and swam across the lake. The echoes of her brothers calls for help confused Finngheal and after swimming several times over and back the lake, her hair fell loose, entangled on her feet and sword and Finngheal was drowned.

The Finn has given up many fine fish in the Urney area with Packie Mc Glinchey and Joe Hunter catching one of the largest fish, a 33lb monster on a boat close to Castlefinn. Fishing on the boats is still a memory to some in the area. The boats were owned by York and O'Flagherty with several 'shots' along the river were the boats could fish. Dealers in Strabane awaited the catch from the boats, sending the fish on to be sold in London. There were also other types of fishing down through the years; however this was more of a nocturnal enterprise using nets, weights and tyre tubes. Each poacher had a 'claim' to his own area on the Finn to put out his net. (This 'claim' would not stand up in court!) Some of these were called "the Drinker", "Killpaddy", and Mosses Sand Bed".

The river Finn was not the only water used for enterprise with the fast flowing water of the Clady burn (back burn) able to drive several scutch mills. The burn was also damned in several places so that flax could be soaked before been sent to the mills. The name Clady burn has come recently into the local history of Urney. No locals ever heard it called Clady burn, nor did I until Dónall Mac Giolla Easpaig of the Placenames Commission was able to verify the name.

Fishing for Salmon on the river Finn
L /R Frank Mc Ghee, Hugh Kelly, Paddy Mc Glinchey, John Mc Goldrick. (Children unknown)

'Shots' on the river Finn from flushtown Bridge.

1. Cesci
2. Flood shot
3. Portmore
4. Back door
5. Phoenix
6. Jet
7. Strone
8. Thone
9. The lower Burnfoot (below Clady bridge)
10. Upper Cesci
11. Landers Wheels
12. Burnfoot
13. Mars
14. The Sand Bed
15. The laga dream
16. Carrick
17. Cevenny
18. Tammy
19. Lower incha
20. Crooked hole (below Castlefinn bridge)
21. Big linta
22. Wee linta
23. Dungorman
24. The Steps

BOATING ON THE FINN

When I rowed up to Clady where the girls are kind and free
My little boat I anchored there, to view the scenery,
A pretty maid in silk arrived, she sprang from wealthy kin,
Invited me to join the spree at Urney, near the Finn.

CHORUS

Boating on the Finn, boys boating on the Finn,
That pretty girl my heart betrayed when boating on the Finn.

She pointed out her home to me, and there we made our way,
I had a hearty lunch with her, likewise a cup of tea!
She introduced me to her da who showed me whips of tin,
That I could act the gentleman and fish the river Finn.

I said I was a stranger and if she would agree,
That I would act as steward for her and assist her with the tea,
She willingly consented, her heart I thought I'd win,
If she didn't turn out slippy like the salmon in the Finn.

The old man got excited and be bade me stop all night,
I tell you we'd some jolly crack till he grew rather tight,
I asked him for the daughter when the little drop was in,
He said, "Young man you're welcome to come live beside the Finn"

Words and music from Denis Phelan who collected them from P. Lennon and Wm. Feery, Clady, Urney, Co. Tyrone.

Roads and bridges of Urney
By Daniel Mc Menamin

Ireland did not begin to get a network of roads until the time of the plantation. Before this, most travel was on horseback with the only roads as such going from the royal seat of Tara to Antrim, Galway, Dublin, Kilkenny, and the fifth towards the North West. The plantation brought with it the need for new roads to aid the free movement of the new settlers between Britain and Ireland and their respective grants of land. In order to do this each parish had to maintain its own network of roads with each man of the parish having to work six days per year with landowners having to provide horse and carts and four men. This system of road building lasted until 1765 when an Irish parliament act replaced the parish system with a tax levied on all citizens for the building of roads and bridges. The bridges built at the time took the shortest route across the rivers and streams, the Flushtown bridge being a good example. This was not too much an inconvenience for the transport of the day, with the cost of materials and labour being the major factor, and the fact that they are still being used today is testament to the quality of the workmanship. It is believed not many bridges were built before 1765 but we do know that some bridge building was taking place from the early 1600's. Inhabitants of County Tyrone were fined £200 pounds for not building a bridge at Castlemoyle beside Newtown around 1628/29 and Construction of the Lifford Bridge had taken place around 1755.

Clady Bridge we know was built sometime before 1754 with twelve pounds, two shillings, and six pence being paid to Rev. Rob Spence and Johnston Mansfield Esq. for repairs to the Bridge on the 4th September 1754. There was further repairs to the bridge in 1767 when fifty three pounds, seventeen shillings, and six pence was paid to Wm Maxwell Esq. for repairs to the bridge consisting of 215 perches of mason work. In 1832, three arches were rebuilt on the bridge with a greater height and span to allow the passing of steamboats.

With Clady being an important fording place going back to the time of O' Neill and O' Donnell, it is possible that a Bridge at Clady was one of the first Bridges on the river Finn. Clady bridge is mentioned in the late 1600's when in 1688 "Colonel Beresford blows up the bridge at Clady to halt Jacobite forces advancing" and in March 1689 the Rev. George Walker "crossed the Finn by the bridge at Clady, which was subsequently destroyed."

The roads network at the beginning of the plantation would have been led by the landlords with the roads connecting the landlords 'big houses' and their land with more roads eventually opening up more land, quarries and bog land. Around 1753 the road from Clady to Castlederg going through Donegal (Drumbane to the top of fern) was being built. The Donegal presentments (assizes) on the 8th Sept 1753 states "We present eighty one pound twelve shillings and six pence to be levied and paid Geo Vaughan Esq. and Wm Cumming to finish new road from Claddy to Derg". In 1786 the road between Urney meeting house and Magheracreggan was built with James Smyth of Magheragar allowed to make 15 perches of road from his house onto the new road.

The estate maps of Conolly Gage (1816) shows the old main road from Castlefinn to Castlederg taking you left towards Alt church through Coolyslin and Cormakilly past the Church and over Gortnagrace. The present Castlederg road was only partially complete with several of the sections stopping and starting at various places eventually joining to give us the winding road we have today. The Skelpy road and Drumdoit road (Magherabrack Road) were not yet connected with the Drumbane to Castlederg road and the Foyfin road was still to be constructed to Dresnagh.

The Urney road which sweeps through "the vale of Urney" was the main stage coach road from Derry to Sligo and was kept in repair by the Grand jury of the Barony of Strabane. The Grand jury consisted mostly of landlords or their agents. Money was given to individuals for the repair and upkeep of roads for a fixed term with the following taken from the summer assizes of 1859:

- "To Roger M'Clenaghan of Robbstown, contract for 5 years, from lent 1858, 1250 perches of mail coach road from Strabane to Claudy between Toal Gallagher's contract and Claudy Bridge".

William Shannon looked after the mail coach road from Strabane to Castlederg (Orchard road) with the following extract:

- "To William Shannon of Ennisclen, contract for five years, from summer 1855, 1608 perches of mail car road from Strabane to Castlederg, between the mail coach road and Ennisclen Bridge".

Stage coaches used to leave Wilson's Hotel travelling through Urney costing eight shillings inside and 1 shilling outside in 1833. The Self Defence, Fair Trader and Royal Mail Car, just some of the names of stage coaches that used the roads.

The landlords of Ireland were able to open up more of their land through the Grand Juries for their own benefit leaving us today with one of the most extensive road networks in the world. Our roads wander leisurely through the countryside, connecting farms to homesteads, old Villages long gone to towns near and far, following the counters of our hills and valleys and many a hard day's work was spent on their construction and repair with the money although hard earned, welcomed by the families around Urney.

Extracts from assizes of County Tyrone

- To John Woods, Sen., of Urney Glebe, contract for 5 years, from lent 1856, 766 perches of road from Castlefinn to Clady between Widow m'Grath's and Patrick m'Aneny's, at 5 ¾d.
- To Manus lafferty of Doneygowan to repair by darning 600 perches of road from Claudy to Newtownstewart, between Andrew Stewart's and Shannon's contract, in the townlands of Claudy, Glentown, Tullymoan and Ennisclen – 300 tons broken stones at 1s. 6d per ton.
- To Solomom Moorehead of Fern, to repair for 5 years 1608 perches of road from Strabane to Castlederg between Enniscleen Bridge and Mr John M'Crea's.
- To Conn Boyle of Somervillestown, contract for 5 years 625 perches from Castlefinn to Newtownstewart between H m'Dade's and Charles Quin's in Somervillestown and Rabstown.
- To Thos. Chambers of Tullymoan, Contract for 2 years from summer 1867, 117 perches of road from Strabane to Castlederg between Claudy Village and the County Donegal, in Claudy and Doneygowan.
- To James Quinn of Glentown, to build a wall 8perches long, 3 feet 6 inches high, 2 feet wide in the townland of Claudy to be completed by 1st Oct 1868.
- To Richard Maxwell Rev. P.B.Maxwell and Andrew Sproull to build an arch on road from Castlefinn to Newtownstewart between Graffy and Lisduff (lisdoo) 1880.

The Wee Donegal
By William Haire

The Londonderry and Enniskillen Railway Company began construction of their railway line in October 1845 to a gauge of 5' 3" from Derry, and they arrived in Strabane by 1847. The line opened for traffic on 19th April 1847, a distance of some 12 miles and was constructed by Leishman. This new form of transport caught the attention of the local landowners in County Donegal, Sir Samuel Hayes and Lord Lifford. They owned considerable portions of land and could see the advantages of this system of transport, as it would provide speedier access to markets with a valuable connection to the Port of Derry. This would increase trade and give a better return for the crops and animals produced on their lands in the Finn Valley area. Preliminary studies were carried out in 1859, with the object of constructing a line between Strabane and Stranorlar. A census was carried out from 10th to the 16th July 1860 between Strabane and Stranorlar with the following traffic being noted as follows:

Vans	12
Carts	909
Jaunting cars	275
Gigs	14
Horses	106
Passengers	2308
Passengers on foot	1105

On 9th September 1861 in the townland of Castletown, a short distance from Strabane station, on land belonging to James Sinclair Esq., Lord Abercorn turned the first sod on a project that would see trains travel through the Finn Valley for near on 100 years. Messrs Moore Brothers had obtained the contract to construct the line and they employed between 600 and 650 men during the construction. Nearing the end of the work Messrs Moore Brothers contacted Anderson and Gormley of Briar Root cottage, with an office at Abercorn square in Strabane, to arrange a dispersal sale of horses in Victoria Market in Londonderry, as they were now surplus due to the line having being completed. The auction date was set for 21st March 1863 at 12 o'clock sharp and buyers could choose from the list below as published on 1st May 1863.

1 Birdy, Black Horse.	10 Blossom, dark Bay Mare.	19 Boxer, Brown Horse.
2 Bell, Chestnut Mare.	11 Johnny, Bay Horse.	20 Switcher, grey Horse.
3 Bobby, Brown Horse.	12 Dandy, Bay Horse.	21 Smiler, Black horse.
4 Bowler, Black Horse.	13 Fanny, Chestnut mare.	22 Mary Anne, Grey Mare.
5 Bowler, Rony Horse	14 Nora, Black Mare.	23 Shamrock, Rony Horse.
6 Major, brown Horse.	15 Sharper, Black Horse.	24 Captain, Bay Horse.
7 Birdy, Black Horse	16 Kate, Black Mare.	25 Sherry, Bay Mare.
8 Rose, Bay Mare.	17 Farmer, Black Horse.	26 Baldy, Black Horse.
9 Dandy, Bay Horse.	18 Jessie, Chestnut Mare.	27 Dandy, Bay Horse.

The line was officially opened on the 7th September 1863 at a total cost of almost £70,000 and was well over budget, using 25,000 native larch sleepers along with 1085 tons of rails. The line from Strabane followed close to the river Finn where it finally left County Tyrone by crossing the Urney Bridge and began its Journey into County Donegal and on to Clady station. It still exists today although it has been unoccupied for a good number of years. From Clady the line wended its way climbing to the next station of Castlefinn, followed by Liscooly, Killygordon and Stranorlar its terminus.

Clady railway station at Cloghfin

The Finn Valley Railway Company had a disappointing start with receipts only half of what had been projected. This was partly caused by the heavy rent extracted by the new owners of Strabane station, the Irish North Western railway company for the use of their station and a bridge over the River Mourne. Despite this the railway continued to expand and in 1892 merged with the West Donegal Railway Company forming the Donegal railway Company (D.R.C). The original Finn Valley Railway was built to the standard gauge of 5' 3", but in 1894 they decided to change the gauge to 3' 0" which was proving to be more suitable for the rural locations served by them, plus a saving in materials and maintenance. The gauge of the West Donegal Railway was 3' 0" so no through traffic could be carried out prior to this without passengers and freight changing trains. On the 13th of July of that year all the staff in the Finn Valley employed by the company were called in to make up all the relaying teams, and they lifted the rail furthest from the platform, it being providential that all stations were built on the near side of the track. They respiked the outer rail to the wooden sleepers and the work was completed by Sunday 15th July, in one weekend with minimal disruption to train services. Because of the high Rent charged for use of Strabane station they also built their own station and bridge across the Mourne.

The Donegal Railway Company owned 75 miles of track by 1895 with lines to Killybegs (1893) and Glenties (1895). The Donegal railway wanted to have their own narrow gauge line from Strabane to Derry to allow free movement of traffic to and from the City of Derry direct from Donegal. This extension was opened for traffic 1st August 1900, with a further extension from Donegal to Ballyshannon opened on 2nd September 1905. The Donegal Railways Company was jointly acquired by the Great Northern Railway of Ireland and the Midland Railway of England in 1906, and the name was changed to County Donegal Railways Joint Committee (CDRJC). The committee was made up of three members from each of the owning companies, but the Derry narrow gauge branch belonged solely to the Midland Railway Company, although the CDRJC worked the branch.

On the 1st, January 1909 the Strabane to Letterkenny section of 19 miles opened, bringing the total mileage up to around 125 miles, thus making this the largest narrow gauge system in the British Isles. The fairs and markets that were held throughout Donegal were a great boost to the railways producing enormous traffic in livestock and people. Many people travelled extensively, some for a day out, with others on business to buy their needs and supplies in towns and villages. Farmers could travel to buy or sell livestock or produce on fair days, where there was a good supply of buyers and commodities on sale.

The Urney Bridge was now over 50 years old and by this stage was in very poor condition, with all drivers warned that there was a maximum speed limit of 10 miles per hour in force, with the time taken to pass over same to be not less than 15 seconds. The old bridge was eventually replaced with a new girder structure between April and September 1924. The partition of Ireland in 1921 led to the creation of custom posts in Strabane, Lifford and Castlefinn. County Donegal was up until then largely supplied from Derry in Northern Ireland and would now have to be supplied mainly from Dublin, due to new duties imposed at the land borders. This led to the use of sealed containers for bonded goods coming from Northern Ireland and these could only be opened by custom officers. The County Donegal Railways had started using a petrol railcar in 1907, first as an inspection car, then later as a means of collecting the morning mails from Glenties. In June 1926 during a coal strike it was used very successfully to this end as it saved sending out a steam train using coal, which was in short supply. The success of this idea paved the way for further railcar development favoured by Henry Forbes after 1926. The railcars were very popular with the travelling public as they could stop almost anywhere on request and were comfortable as well.

The 1940's saw the beginning of the end of the railway as spiralling cost in wages, coal and severe competition from road transport, the growth of private cars, and a public now not using the railway to the same extent reduced profit to almost nothing. Capital was not available to replace worn rails and life expired sleepers as both the owning companies were suffering major losses in their receipts as well. An application for complete closure of the railway was made in May 1959. On 31st of December 1959 locomotive no 5 Drumboe driven by Mr James Mc Menamin with his brother Frank as fireman, left Strabane station with people on the platform singing "The Last Train To San Fernando", passing over Urney bridge and up the Finn valley in pouring rain for the last time. The train arrived at Stranorlar at 8:21pm completing its Finn Valley journey, as had all trains since the line was opened, but this was its last official passenger duty, as all traffic would now be transferred to substitute road services for both passengers and freight.

A railway scene from Castlefinn.

The major task of lifting the track began in March 1960, after which rail, sleepers, wagons, carriages, locomotives and plant were auctioned off. Local farmers eagerly bought many of the wagons for storage purposes. A few of the carriages were bought for holiday homes. An American, Dr Ralph Cox, of Wildwood, New Jersey, purchased steam locomotives Meenglass, Drumboe, Erne and Columbkille, railcars 12,14,16 and 18 , 10 coaches, 20 covered wagons, 20 wagon chassis plus 100 tons of rails and fastenings, 10 tons of points and signalling rods, Stranorlar signal cabin and turntable, a small 18ft turntable plus the veranda roof from Stranorlar station. Steam locomotives Alice and Lydia were sold for scrap along with railcars 14 and 15. The steel bridges along the system all went for scrap. Dr Cox's ambitious plan to set up a railway in America came to nothing as shipping costs and his own circumstances changed, with all of the stock remaining in Ireland. After a number of years Erne built 1904 was cut up at Letterkenny, but some stock at Strabane fared much worse as all of the carriages were reduced to underframes. The timberwork was systematically stripped and burned, with only locomotives Meenglass and Drumboe and some underframes surviving. The unofficial scrap men stole all parts of any value of these two steam engines before they were rescued by The North West of Ireland Railway Society in Derry.

The Wee Donegal as it had become affectionately known had been used by many people living in the Finn Valley during its long existence. The special excursions using the steam trains were numerous and many a great day was had at the Glenties Harvest Fair, a day trip to Bundoran with its famous amusements and beach, or a very popular Rossnowlagh with its long golden strand which stretches for miles on the flat. The train carried children to school, men, women and children went to Strabane to be hired at the hiring fairs, and many more parted from their families leaving these shores for a new home in America in search of a better life. Local folk used the train as a telephone to send messages down the line for a doctor or vet. It was also a great way to check your time, as generally it was never late. Farmers could arrange to stop for their tea if working in the field, and delighted children knew school was over for another day, when they heard the train whistling as it approached the station. Today you can still see traces of our railway past; the supports for Urney Bridge, hedges which enclosed the railway can be seen in parts from Killygordon right through to Barnesmore where a stone overbridge can be seen at the side of the road, a tribute to the skills of the stone masons of that time. The various railway station buildings at Clady, Castlefinn and Killygordon still exist to this day but are now in private ownership.

PRESERVATION OF COUNTY DONEGAL RAILWAY STOCK
In 1991 the formation of Cumann Traenach na Gaeltacht Lair took place, and with the aid of a FAS scheme they started to relay track on part of the original track. They started from Fintown station, on the original Glenties line along the shores of Lough Finn. The Fintown Railway as it is now called, is run as a train service using railcar 18.

The COUNTY DONEGAL RAILWAY RESTORATION LIMITED.
In Donegal Town, at the former railway station, a museum has been set up and run by County Donegal Railway Restoration Limited (CDRRL) where a small group have made sterling work of collecting and restoring historic railway vehicles and related items. A large photographic image collection of the railway when originally running is complied on the premises for consultation. Steam locomotive Drumboe a 2-6-4T built 1907 is at present being restored to working order with major work already done, but it requires more money and work before it returns to work in Donegal to earn a living within the next few years. Coach 28 built 1893 by Oldbury Carriage

and Wagon Company has been restored and sits outside the museum where it is currently receiving a repaint at present and looks magnificent in its cream and red livery protecting it from Donegal winters. Many tickets also survive in a variety of colours and types, to show the journeys possible last century and at prices which would not apply today if the line was operational.

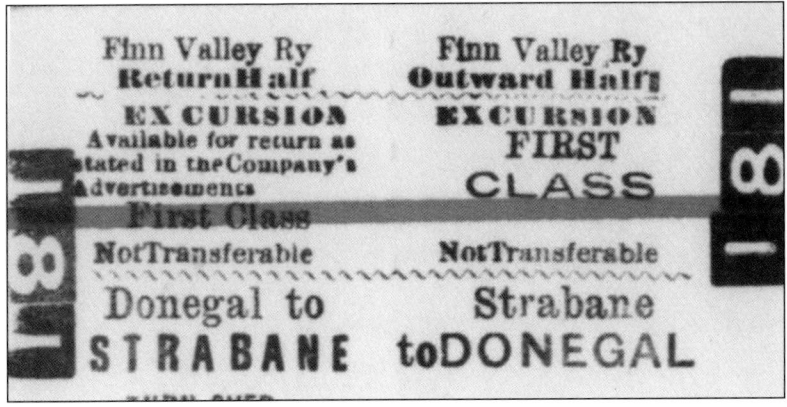

Finn Valley Railway ticket Donegal to Strabane.

The ISLE OF MAN RAILWAY COMPANY.

At the auction of the CDRJC rolling stock after closure, The Isle of Man Railway Company purchased the newest railcars, numbers 19 and 20, having been built in 1950 and 1951 respectively and in perfect running order. They were built by GNR(I) in Dundalk & Walker Brothers of Wigan. They still exist on The Isle of Man, but are undergoing a complete rebuild at the present on the island, and will return to service on completion of this painstaking job.

The FOYLE VALLEY RAILWAY.

Most of the rolling stock purchased by Dr Cox was preserved and rescued by The North West of Ireland Railway Society, and can now be seen in the Railway Museum at the city end of Craigavon Bridge. This museum is open during summer months and is run by Derry City Council and is well worth a visit to inspect this unique collection of C.D.R. stock.

The ULSTER FOLK and TRANSPORT MUSEUM CULTRA

This museum houses a large collection of Irish railway vehicles with the County Donegal stock well represented. One part of the collection Railcar number 1 was the first combustion engine railway vehicle in Ireland, and among the pioneers of such traction in the world. It's use paved the way for diesel traction and it could be claimed that this small vehicle is the mother of all our modern diesel trains in the world at large as it proved its viability and an economy unseen before this vehicle ran.

A standard open wagon in grey livery stands on rails here unlikely to have its paint marked by goods in transit. Much of the signalling equipment from Castlefinn signal box is on display here, along with the interchange sign from Strabane platform, proudly proclaiming that you must change here from the broad gauge to get a connection on The Donegal lines, to your destination station on the narrow gauge.

CONCLUSION

Much has survived of the Donegal Railway stock and is in secure ownership, but a lot remains to be done to protect the exhibits not yet restored from further damage due to age. Why don't you visit some of these museums, and see for yourself these priceless historic collections of our own railway heritage. The railway although closed for fifty years has not been forgotten completely, as these items are a living reminder of a once proud railway system, that served Donegal folk faithfully for almost a century. The complete story has been well documented by DR. Edward M. Patterson and this article is dedicated to the men involved in the construction and all of the staff who worked on the railway. They overcame many problems and obstacles in a changing world, led by excellent General Managers. Alas now a distant event in our older generations memories, with many of our younger folk never having seen or travelled on a Donegal train.

Landlords

By Daniel Mc Menamin

An absentee landlord who left the running of his estate in the hands of an agent was not known to have the welfare of his tenants at heart. For this reason, Sir James Galbraith of Urney Park as the only landlord in the Urney area who lived on his estate would have been well liked by the majority of his tenants. A letter sent to Galbraith thanking him for a dinner he had laid on for some of his tenants was signed by A. Sproule Tullymoan, William Inch Inchenny, Thomas Baird Inchenny and Wm M'laughlin. As well as owning land in Tyrone, he also owned the Townlands of Cloghfin and Ballylast. He died on 8th May 1827 with Lady Galbraith passing away on 14th May 1842. The Next owners of Urney Park and its lands was Andrew F. Knox with Mr John Callison as his land Stewart. The land was put up for sale on 11th November 1865, however in 1875 the reps of Andrew and Thomas Knox still held 1231 acres.

The Gage family owned the Manor of Castlefinn from 1694 until 1892. There was a partnership between Conolly McCausland and Hodson Gage in the running of the Manor but it eventually became the property of the Gage family. On the 8th February 1752, there was an agreement that Hodson Gage would pay a bond of £1,035, the remaining sum due for the purchase of the Manor of Castlefinn. The Gage family lived at Bellarena, Co Derry. Marcus Gage was the landlord by 1814 handing it on to his son Conolly soon afterwards. Conolly Gage had Finn Lodge built sometime before 1836. This house which still stands today as a farm shed in Cavanawerry was also called Fyfinn lodge, Finn Cottage and Cavanawerry lodge. Gage, as a non-resident landlord must have used the cottage only occasionally. He encouraged his tenants to reclaim land allowing them "so much per perch for fencing, limestone and turf to burn it". In 1851; Sir Frederick Heygate had taken over the running of the Manor when he married Marianne Gage, the heiress to both the Bellerna and Castlefinn estates.

Finn Lodge, former residence of Conolly Gage

Urney Park

OTHER LANDLORDS

There were several small landlords in the Urney area. A family called Brown seems to have had a Freehold on Millfarm and Magherycallaghan. This was later taken over by James Mc Curdy. Mc Curdy is believed to have built the embankment along the river at Magherycallaghan as a famine relief project. A Dr. Finton owned Mullanboy with a Mr Browne landlord of Gortnagrace and the rector of Donaghmore was the landlord of Calhame and Alt Upper.

Rev William Knox who was the rector of Clonleigh parish, was the landlord of several townlands including Bellspark, Inchenny Upper, Glentown and Rabstown. He was the Father of Andrew F. Knox of Urney Park. The Rev. Peter B. Maxwell also held five townlands, Skerryglass, Hunterstown, Donnygowan, Lisdoo and Tullymoan. Rev. Maxwell lived at Birdstown, Buncrana and was the rector of Desertegny.

Magherycallaghan house

Urney Players
By Johnny Corry

THE Urney Players were formed quite by chance, FERGUS CLEARY, who was entertainment officer at St Conals Hospital Letterkenny, asked Mary Ellen Mc Cauley if she could get a few people to take part in a concert he was organising in Burt, so we gathered up a few and went to the concert, while there he suggested that we enter a competition in Letterkenny called 'TOPS OF THE TOWN', we had never heard of it, but we had a meeting and decided to have a go. Much to our surprise we got through to the quarter finals, and won best production and fifty pounds, a fortune back then and so began a decade of show business and for the village, practically every family in Clady were involved along with people in Doneyloop, and rehearsals were in Flannigan's Lounge. At this time the troubles were at their height and a really FORTIFIED CHECK POINT WAS INSTALLED IN CLADY.

Molloy's All Star Band, Clady.
L-R Willie Molloy, Patsy Molloy, Loughlin Mc Glinchey(singer), Paddy Mc Cauley, Billy Barr, Patsy Molloy, Mickey Christie.

We had sixty or seventy people from fifteen years upwards, gathering two or three times a week for rehearsals, and praise to the young people there was never a clash between the army and us, and it wasn't for want of provocation, during that ten years, we won best production four times, plus many other credits. It wasn't just the stars who were appearing on stage which made the show, the people in the background making costumes painting scenery and raising funds, and particular Rosie Langan RIP who was dresser confidante and mother to everyone, also Mrs Mary Nelis and Mrs Mc Corkell RIP who made the costumes. No show was complete without the musicians who backed the show over the years.

Another aspect of this time we played host to St Conal's patients , having them visit us for an afternoon each year this was an inspirational time for us, and again our young people took part, talking to and dancing with the patients. At that time we had moved to Kirks bar in Cloghfin, all in all it was a great accolade from 1975 to 1989, and it is still talked about with fondness in Clady.

Jimmy Houston

Jimmy Houston was born in Skelpy Upper around 1929. Jimmy loved music and began to play the fiddle at fourteen years, travelling to Spamount to be taught by Jonny Dunphy. He was soon in demand for dances and house parties around Urney with one party in Drumnaha still well remembered for the quality of the music when Jimmy was still in his teens. Jimmy met his wife Mary (nee Mc Kinney, Alt) when they were at Alt school. Jimmy would have known and played with many notable fiddle players and singers in the area, John Mc Glinchey, a fiddle player from Gortnamuck, and Hugh Dooher, a great singer originally from Donemana who lived in Calhame. Other notable musicians in the area at the time were the Molloy's of Clady and the McPhilemy's of Castlefinn. Job prospects were not great at that time in the area, and so, Jimmy left for work in Scotland in 1949. He soon returned to Ireland and in 1958; he won the fiddle competition in the first Fleadh Cheoil in Co Donegal. He was a member of the Tirconaill Ceili band Crossroads, playing all over Donegal as well competing in a number of All Ireland's. Jimmy Houston is well remembered around the area to this day for his love of Irish music and the generosity in which he shared it with others.

School Days in Urney

By Daniel Mc Menamin

Most of the schools in the early 1800s were pay schools with the teaching taking place in a rented cottage or barn. Students paid a sum to the teacher from 1s – 1d per quarter in the case of Alt Upper up to 1s – 6d per quarter in Drumdoit with additional support from the Kildare place society, the rector and some landlords. The Marquis of Abercorn contributed to schools at Sion and Tullywhisker. Catholic schools were only beginning to emerge from the hedges around Urney and mostly existed without financial support.

The national Education Act of 1831 was welcomed by the Catholic hierarchy and later by the Presbyterian Assembly, but the Church of Ireland was divided on the act. The new education system, designed to be non denominational had the opposite effect. Pressure from church leaders and politicians led to changes with the system which still reverberates today, leaving us with a system of education based mainly on religious denomination.

The statistical report by Lieutenant Wilkinson (1836) tells us of six schools in the area. One at Urney Glebe had 95 students with two teachers, John Crowe and Jane Gwynne. Alt Upper had 45 students with Francis Mc Divett getting paid £13 10 shillings per Annum. Another at Alt Upper beside the Church had 57 students with a William Katerson (Catterson) in charge. A school at Drimdoit (Drumdoit) With John Elliot as headmaster had 34 students, Andrew Smiley was the master in charge at Tullywhisker with 113 students and Sion with 128 students was looked after by M. Wade. The report lists reading, writing and arithmetic as the main educational subjects at that time. Tullywhisker School was built in 1822. Another school at Rabstown had 44 students in 1855.

The Griffith valuation of 1858 mentions the school at Roganspark under the stewardship of the Church Education Society. This society was set up by the Church of Ireland as a preferred option to the national schools act of 1831. Alt Upper also had a night school which taught children that had to work on the family farm during the day.

In 1906 Rev. J McElhatton applied for a grant to build a new school at Clady to take the place of Ballybogen School two miles away. Students from Clady at that time went to school at Rabstown or Ballybogen with children often using the pile bridge as a short cut to Ballybogen. The new school was sanctioned on the 25th January 1908, however the Clady school was to 'supersede' two schools, Ballybogen and Alt no 1 School (now St Safans). Opposition to the closure of both schools started immediately with large maps of the area produced showing the distances each student would have to travel to Clady. On 24th January 1911, Mr E.J. Kelly, M.P. for the area sent a letter to the department pleading for the retention of the school. A letter of protest was also sent signed by the parents of the children attending Alt. Charles Doherty of Drumdoit, John Clarke of Cormakilly, Philip Gallen of Gortnagrace and John Rush of Alt, just some of the signatories of the letter. On the opening of Clady School in 1912, Ballybogen school closed its doors, with Alt given a reprieve no doubt because of local anger. The first principal of Clady school was Mr Joseph Reid.

Clady National School Built 1912

The Principal of Alt School was Bridget A. Feely who boarded with Rebecca O'Flaherty and her daughters in Clady Village. She was replaced by Miss Jane Kerr on 15th January 1912. Three schools remain in the Urney area, One at Ballylast which opened on 25th April 1955, St Marys national school, Clady replacing the school of 1912 opened in 1967 and St Safans national school, Drumdoit which opened in 1994 replacing Alt Lower. (Alt Lower was opened in 1934 replacing an earlier school on the same site.)

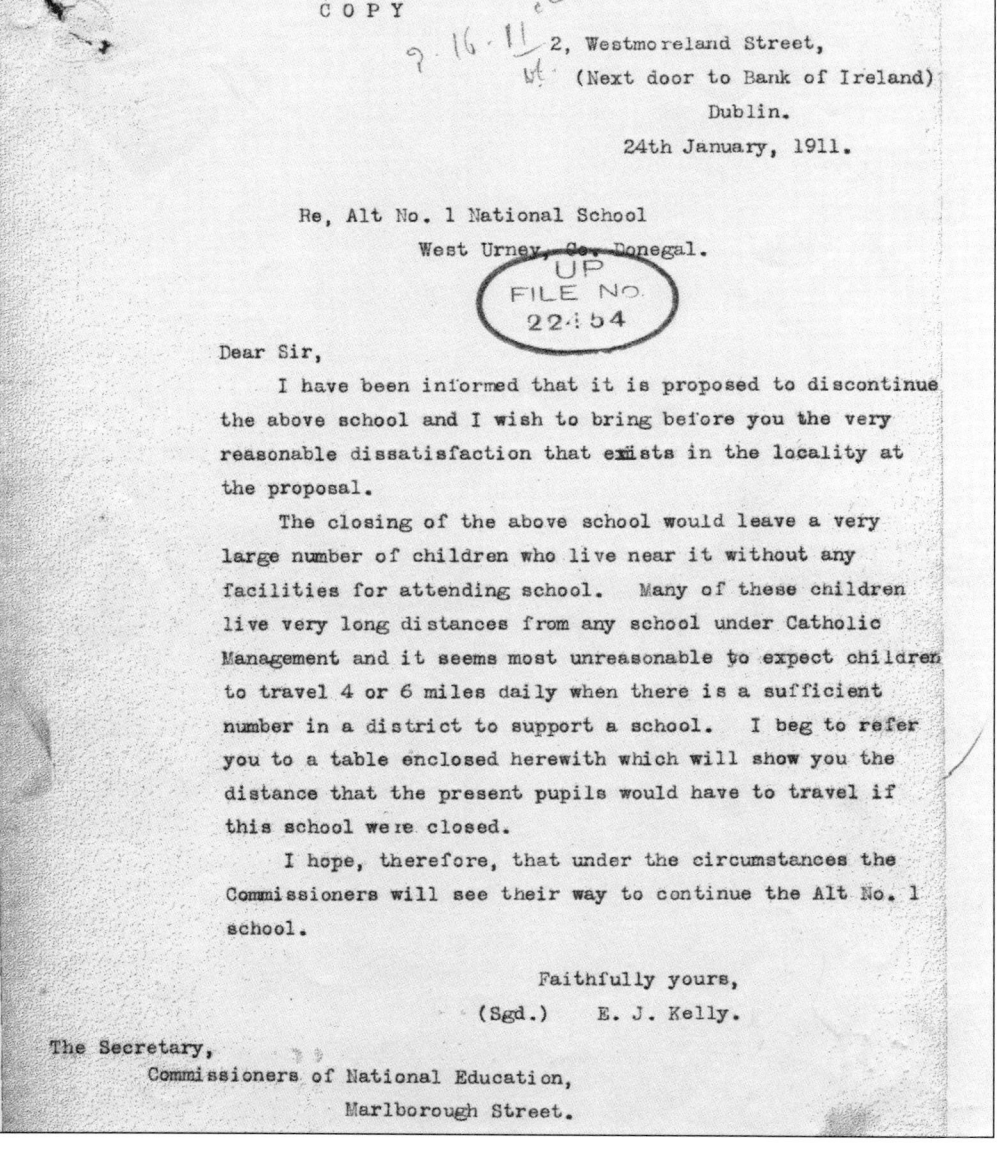

Letter from E.J. Kelly Looking for Alt Lower school to remain open

Schools within a radius of three miles from Clady - 1909			
School	Average Attendance	Average on school rolls	Religious Denomination
Ballybogen	36	61	Catholic
Alt (1)	20	41	Catholic
Alt (2)	19	64	Presbyterian
Urney (1)	44	105	Presbyterian
Urney (2)	26	45	Church of Ireland
Castlefinn Boys	38	57	Catholic
Castlefinn Girls	60	58	Catholic
Castlefinn (2)	36	86	Methodist
Sion Mills Boys	111	100	Church of Ireland
Sion Mills Girls	102	100	Church of Ireland
Rabstown	51	48	Catholic

A LOOK AT THE INSPECTORS BOOK _ 1869 – 1912

1869 - 29 children present, exercise books should be used instead of slate

1879 - Out offices need to be cleared out

1882 - A large map of the world needed

1885 - Only 26 present owing to farm work

1886 - Teacher permits children to copy and count on their fingers

1887 - Pupils much too noisy

1888 - Children whisper answers to each other

1889 - White wash throughout is needed

1891 - Pupils should come to school early, I passed 9 or10 playing on the road.

1895 - Pupils restless and talkative

1904 - Children allowed to spit on the floor

1906 - One boy sent on a message to Clady. Not to be repeated.

1909 - School was cold, several pains of glass broken.

1911 - Children are nicely mannered, poor attendance, neglected appearance.

1912 - Slates should be discontinued.

Alt Lower school opened 1934

Tullywisker school opened 1910

Ballylast National School in the 1950's

Children at Ballylast National School in the late 1950's

Children from Clady national school on their first Communion day 1927

Our Country

Like a king fallen from grace,
your down upon your knees.
Waiting for you to rise again,
to put our minds at ease.

A future so uncertain now,
It can bring some to tears.
Sleepless nights and tortured dreams,
as we realise our fears.

You were once a strong empire,
like a wild flower you did grow.
And no-one foreseen the danger, no
nobody was to know.

Though now it may seem hopeless, and
I've watched in disbelief.
But I believe in my country and,
someday soon we'll find relief.

She'll someday soon conquer darkness,
and reach her destination.
This she must believe in firmly,
shemust find an explanation.

Her spirit is relentless, her heart has
come through fire
She will not stop till her soul is free,
She'll take it to the wire.

Priscilla Mc Kinney
Drumdoit.

Urney - History / People / Place

The Ballad of Bella Brooks

Ye tender hearted Christians I hope you will draw near,
And listen to these mournful lines I mean to let you hear,
Concerning a foul murder that occurred some years ago,
And how the crime was perpetrated I mean to let you know.

Being about three miles from Castlefin in the County Donegal,
There lived a farmer's daughter; she was handsome, young and tall.
She used to receive some visits from another farmer's son,
And he being sly and cunning too, her favour soon he won.

He kept this fair one's company for a long space of time,
The pubic accused him' Guilty!' of that inhuman crime.
She had given him £200 the people do tell me,
And when he robbed her of her life was allowed to go free.

Little did this fair one know he was so hard of heart,
She thought that they would soon be wed, on earth no more to part.
She listened to and believed each word the horrid wretch did say,
When he told her pleasant stories of their approaching wedding day.

This man had no intention for to make her his wife,
But he had still intended to end her youthful life.
No sooner did this wretched man the simple maid betray,
Then he contrived some wicked means to take her life away.

He took her to his father's house, there awhile to keep,
One night he gave the chloroform which caused her for to sleep.
And when he got her sleeping he went to his servant boy,
For to propose some wicked means her life for to destroy.

He got her upon a trap, between him and his servant man,
And they hurried on to execute their violent wicked plan
There were no neighbours near the spot, nor yet one kindly friend,
To save this maid so innocent from such and untimely end.

These two cold-blooded murderers sped on with lightening speed,
Until they reached the spot they were to commit their evil deed.
They drew close to the water and cruelly threw her in,
Next day her lifeless body was discovered in the Finn.

They took her out of the water and stretched her on the shore,
They saw human aid was useless, her life for to restore.
The police were summoned and the news soon spread around,
The neighbours were all shocked to hear that Bella Brooks was drowned.

This fair one was an orphan, her parents had passed away,
No doubt had they been still alive they would have looked for fair play.
They would have him arrested by who she was betrayed,
They would have had him tried and punished for the murder of their child.

Both the doctor and the coroner were bribed we do believe,
To cloak this guilty murder and the public to deceive.
The Lord is just and merciful; he will not suffer long,
He'll punish all that cloaked this murder and that before long.

This wretched man is still alive but miserable he must feel,
Endeavouring from the eye of man his guilt for to conceal.
But he won't conceal it from the Lord, who knows our secrets all,
And if we violate his laws his wrath will on us fall.

This wretched and unhappy man no comfort can he find,
The thoughts of this cruel murder still torments his mind.
He knows he's guilty of the crime and the time is drawing near,
When he must render strict account of this wretched wild career.

Urney Oats

The heart O corn, for such it is
To fortify to build
These mortal bodies of us all
They will our stomachs fill.

In boyhood and in mans estate
We watch from the wayside growing
The summer sun makes the ripened grain
We reap because of sowing.

It's for you it comes today
From Irelands finest fields
The combine separates from the straw
The mill makes into meal.

We take with breakfast if we're wise
For dessert what could be better
For supper it's the only food
From all disease to fetter.

Now I'll name this precious gem
Forgive me if I quote
For taste, for food, for energy
Sure it's Maxwell Urney Oats

Thomas Semple

The Hunterstown Ghost

There are those who will remember
Especially in north Tyrone
Of a ghost over a hundred years ago
That was active in Tullymoan.

It's in the district once again
Been seen about and around
But it's slightly misjudged it's place
And turned up in Hunterstown.

It knocks at windows, rattles doors
In the field disturbs the herd
It hurled a heavy stone one night
Into the yard of Thomas Baird.

It visited the home of a decent man
And threatened to put in his roof
With a bombardment of Scotstown rock
That naughty elusive spook.

Next call to a house in Hunterstown
The whole family will swear the same
With the clock on the table go'an for twelve
A hand through the window came.

The mother with fright fainted over
Within her arms a baby
By the time I got out say John
That spook was hitting Clady.

To catch this ghost came a noted athlete
And footballer by name O'Kane
Five feet was as near as he could get
Then it fled like an express train.

Some residents claim to have seen it
And crowds have come in cars by night
It may leave soon these Urney towns
And to some other clime take flight.

Thomas Semple

Photos of Clady come from The Cooper collection taken around 1912

Urney - History / People / Place

The Magherycallaghan Ghost

Magherycallaghan is a lovely place,
That's free from noise and din,
Beside old Clady Village,
Not far from Castlefinn.

And tourists on the roadway,
Can view the Elm trees,
How their crooked branches dance and sway,
Before the western breeze.

Close by there is an orchard,
Where the apples first get ripe,
There are pear trees and plum trees,
And trees of every type.

The avenue is delightful,
With its flowers on every side,
And the mighty "Castle" all to see,
Stands looking down with pride.

It was a country residence,
For fifty years or more,
Of a captain bold as Sam told,
Who drove in a coach and four.

And it is haunted by a ghost,
As most all people know,
Supposed to be some murdered man,
Long dreary years ago.

That was like man with sword in hand,
One dismal winters night,
When after some hard fighting,
Put the highway man to flight.

But one of them lay wounded,
One of the robbers band,
And he was hanged upon a tree,
At the Captains stern command.

And since that night his Ghost appears,
As most all people say,
Beside the tunnel entrance,
To chase earthly men away.

One night he struck big Charlie Leitch,
And down big Charlie fell,
Like Lucifer descending,
To the burning pits of hell.

Charlie lay quite senseless,
For but a space of time,
When at last he said the ghost he blamed,
For this inhuman crime.

The next he struck was Donal Rogan,
Who fell and broke his knee,
He did go down stern for most,
Like a sinking ship at sea.

How to conclude and finish,
I've got one word to say,
That any man with awkward feet,
From the ghost should keep away.

Composed by John Burns
Ballybogan
Lifford.

William Burke

By Daniel Mc Menamin

William Burke was born in Urney in 1792 to poor but well respected parents. He joined the Donegal Militia serving as an officer's servant for five years. During this time he met and married a girl from Ballina, Co Mayo having two children, none of whom lived. Around 1817 leaving his wife behind, he emigrated to Scotland getting a job on the union canal. It was at this time he fell in with a girl called Helen Mc Dougal. When the canal was finished he and Mc Dougal lived in Peebles and Leith where he worked at various jobs before moving to Edinburgh. In November 1827 he met Margaret Laird who introduced them to her common law husband William Hare a fellow Ulster man(Derry or Newry), who kept a lodging house in Tanners close, West Port. They had a drink and Hare offered a room to Burke and Mc Dougal.

In December 1827 a lodger named Donald died owing £4 rent to Hare. To recoup his money Hare proposed that they sell the body to Edinburgh medical college and share the earnings, the college needing fresh bodies to train medical students. They took the body from the coffin, filled it with tanner's bark and hid the body under the bed. They went to the yard of the college where a student referred them instead to Dr Knox's private medical school. They brought the body to Dr Knox's room and on checking the body the Dr authorised a man called Jones to pay Burke and Haire £7 and 10 shillings. Jones made it clear that they would take any other bodies that may come their way. The easy money to be made was to start Burke and Hare off on a murderess journey that would end with William Hare turning Kings Evidence and the execution of William Burke.

By the time the duo was caught on Saturday November 1st 1828 they had murdered and sold the bodies of 16 more victims to Dr Knox. First they preyed on sick lodgers from Hare's house, getting them drunk on whiskey, they then murdered the victim with one holding the nose and mouth of the victim and the other holding down the body. This became their trademark method of killing their victims as it left no marks on the bodies to raise suspicions. Burke and Hare then moved on to enticing their victims off the street for drink or a bed for the night.

Burke and Hare murdered among others a man called Joseph who was sick at the time, a prostitute Mary Patterson, Elizabeth Haldane and a few months later her daughter Peggy and an old Irish women and her grandson. Mary Patterson was murdered in the home of Constantine Burke, William Burke's brother. The pair were paid between £8 and £10 pounds for their murderous deeds.

Another of their victims was a young man called James Wilson better known as Daft Jimmy. He was well known in the West Port area having a deformed foot and low intellect. He was recognised by students in Dr Knox's anatomy class. Dr Knox denied it was Daft Jimmy and immediately began dissecting his face. Hare claimed at the trial that it was Burke who was the main culprit in Daft Jimmy's murder, but in a letter of confession Burke wrote on the week before his execution, "Concerning Daft Jimmy I declare that Wm. Hare was the first that laid hands on him"

Burke and Hare's last victim was a woman called Mary Docherty who is believed to have hailed from Donegal. Burke met Docherty in a shop and enquiring about her name claimed that his mother was also Docherty and that they were related. Burke and Mc Dougal had at this stage moved into their own place in Portsbourgh, offered Docherty a bed and supper for the night (Friday 31st October 1828).

William Burke born in Urney, 1792

Ann and James Gray had been lodging with Burke for a number of days. Burke needing to get rid of them for the night sent them to Hares house and promised to pay for their lodging and breakfast. That night Burke and Hare murdered Mary Docherty and after stripping her, covered her body with straw at the bottom of a bed in Burke's house. The Grays became suspicious when Docherty was nowhere to be seen the next morning. Burke had also warned Ann Gray not to go near the bottom of the bed were she had left stockings. The Grays on having been left alone in the house that evening checked the straw and found the body of Docherty. On their way to alert police they met Mc Dougal who offered them £10 per week for their silence. They refused and alerted the police which brought to an end Burke and Hare's murderous enterprise and making William Burke Urney's most infamous Export.

The evidence against the pair was not strong as they had time to bring the body to the college before the police had arrived. Hare and Laird were offered their freedom if they testified against Burke and Mc Dougal. The trial started on Christmas Eve 1828 and with the help of Hare's testimony Burke was found guilty and was sentenced to be hanged. The case against Mc Dougal was "not proven" by the jury and on hearing this Burke turned to Mc Dougal and said "Nelly, you are out of the scrape".

Burke resigned to his fate, made a full confession stating that when growing up in Urney "his mind was under the influence of religious impressions and that he was accustomed to read his Catechism and his Prayer-book". A paper of the time wrote "He fully acknowledges the justice of his sentence; nay, he considers it in some measure as a blessing, the certainty of his approaching fate having brought back his mind to a sense of religion"

On Wednesday the 28th January 1829 in front of a crowd of some 25,000 people, William Burke was hanged to the cries of "BURKE HIM HANG HIM". His Body was given to Edinburgh medical college where it was used just like his victims in anatomy lectures. Burke's skeleton, death mask and a book bound in his skin are on display at the Royal College of surgeon's museum. From the method of murder used by Burke and Hare the word "burke" was introduced to the English dictionary.

To Burke: To murder by suffocation, or so as to produce few marks of violence, for the purpose of obtaining a body to be sold for dissection.

William Hare was released and headed south to England where as one story goes his identity was discovered by a mob who threw him into a lime pit. He is rumoured to have spent his final days a blind beggar in London dying in 1859.

Helen Mc Dougal returned to West Port to be met with an angry mob. She is rumoured to have left for Australia and is reported to have died in August 1868 in a house fire at Singleton, New South Wales.

Margaret Laird returned to Ireland never to be heard of again.

Dr Knox Never talked about the murders. After failing to get employment at the medical schools in Edinburgh he moved to London getting a job at the cancer hospital. He died there in 1862.

Honest John Kelly

For many generations Ireland's best export has been its people. We send some of our best young people off for the benefit of other countries to the detriment of our own. The political and economic landscape of the U.S.A. may have been a lot different if not for the likes of the Kennedy clan or Henry Ford. It was politics that benefited from the emigration of Hugh Kelly and his wife Sarah. Hugh was born on the Tyrone Donegal border where his family had a small farm in Graffy. He met and married Sarah Donnelly (Fermanagh) and because of a lack of opportunities in Ireland, they decided to emigrate to New York around 1815. This was not an easy decision to make, for many it meant never seeing one's family again.

Their son John was born on 20th April, 1822 and when his Father Hugh died in 1830, John had to leave school to support his family. He got a job as an apprentice grate setter and stone cutter, eventually setting up his own business in which he was very successful. Between 1837 and 1842 John was involved in the defence of St Patricks Cathedral against the 'The Native American Party' and 'The no Nothing Party'. He entered politics in 1850 and in 1856 he became the only Catholic in the U.S. house of representatives at that time. After the death of his wife and only son he retired from politics and travelled Europe with his two daughters.

Honest John Kelly

On his return to New York, political corruption from within had crippled Tammany hall and Kelly was persuaded to take over its leadership. Tammany hall was the Democratic Party political machine which played a major part in controlling politics in New York City. With the influx of millions of Irish immigrants after the great famine, "Tammany hall is forever linked with the rise of the Irish in American politics". Kelly purged Tammany of its corrupt leader William Tweed and his associates introducing respectable democrats as members. In 1876 Kelly married Theresa Mullan, niece of Cardinal McCloskey, Cardinal of New York. In 1886, suffering from ill health for several years John Kelly, the son of an Urney immigrant died.

Kelly got the name 'Honest John Kelly from his period in Tammany hall when getting rid of its corrupt leadership. The wallsteads of John's father Hugh still stand today, with some of Honest Johns family now living in Inchenny and Derry.

Tobias Mullen

Tobias Mullen was born in Urney on the 4th March 1818, the youngest of six sons to James and Mary (nee Travers). Patrick, James and Robert were the names of three of his brothers. Locals tell of the Mullen family living in the 'pound house' outside of Clady. He obtained his early education at a school in Castlefinn before moving to Maynooth College where he studied theology. In 1843 he accepted an invitation to join the Diocese of Pittsburgh, Pennsylvania by Bishop Michael O'Conner where he completed his theological studies and was ordained to the priesthood on the 1st Sept 1844. A chance meeting between a group of Sisters of Mercy and the young Tobias en route to America was to have an effect on education for young women years later in Pennsylvania as we will see. Tobias served as curate at the Cathedral of Pittsburgh for about two years, afterwards taking charge of congregations at Johnstown and Jefferson County. In 1854 he was transferred to the rectorship of St. Peter's Church at Allegheny and served as vicar general of the Diocese of Pittsburgh from 1864 to 1868.

Pound House, Clady

On the 3rd March 1868 Tobias was appointed the third Bishop of Erie by pope Pius IX. During his time as bishop of Erie, many priests were ordained, parishes established and churches built. He also founded the Catholic weekly *Lake Shore Visitor*, an orphanage, and two hospitals. Bishop Mullen, on remembering the chance meeting with the Sisters of Mercy, invited them to Erie in 1870 in order to set up a Catholic school for girls. In 1871, the Order opened Saint Joseph Academy, a private school for girls in Titusville, Pennsylvania. Bishop Mullen's greatest accomplishment was the erection of St. Peter's Cathedral dedicated in 1893. The Cathedral was originally dubbed "Mullen's folly". Bishop Mullen had a stroke on the 20th May 1897 and remained in ill health until his death on 22nd April 1900

MASTER ROBERT

On Friday the 28th of March 1924, a 25-1 rank outsider "Master Robert" shocked many by winning the Aintree Grand National, Master Robert was not your usual Grand National winner, a towering horse of chestnut colour standing a full 17 hands high and it was stated at the time, He was "more of a hunter type than a racehorse". The horse was bred by Robert Mc Kinlay of Sessamore, Castlefinn on his farms at Castlefinn and Stephenstown, Clady. No better person to tell the story of Master Robert than Robert himself who recounted the following story in the 1924 Bloodstock Breeders Review;

"It does not fall to the lot of many men to breed a Grand National winner on his first attempt at breeding thoroughbreds as in my case of breeding Master Robert. A short history of Master Robert's mother, Dodds, may not be out of place. Dodds, as a foal, was sent, along with some older horses, by her breeder, Mr. Dodds, of Hamilton, near Glasgow, to be wintered in Ireland. Dodds was a very weakly foal, so weak that for a long time after she came over, when she lay down she was unable to rise without assistance. When Mr. Dodds returned the next spring to take his horses home he found the filly with a deformity in one of his hind legs, and, considering her not worth taking back, made a present of her to the late Mr. Robert Patterson, of Manor Cunningham, Co, Donegal, who had been keeping the animals for him. When Dodds grew up Patterson bred several foals from her, all fillies, and whether they were not well enough done I can't say, but they did not grow to much size, and all went to the army as troopers.

"Patterson decided not to breed any more pure-bred foals off her, and at that time I had a Clydesdale stallion. He mentioned to me that he was going to put her to my Clydesdale. I demurred, and advising sticking to the thoroughbred with her, but he was determined not to breed any more thoroughbreds. After a considerable argument with him I made a proposal that he should lend Dodds to me to breed a foal, and to this he readily assented. The mare thereupon came to my place, and was put to Moorside II. The result was Master Robert.

"When Master Robert was born he was an enormous size, almost twice the size of a normal foal. He grew like a mushroom, and so, as a yearling, was very big. When he was two years old I sent him to Mr. Maurice Reidy, at the Curragh, who kept him for a time, and, honest gentleman that he is, wrote to me what coincided exactly with my own opinion of the colt – that he was too much overgrown, and although fast, could not get quickly enough into his stride to compete against other two-year-olds more matured and of less growth. Reidy advised me to take him home until he was five years old and make a 'chaser' of him. I brought him home and had him cut. As my son was at that time in France, and I was away from home all the time, I had no one to look after Master Robert properly or exercise him, so I thought a little ploughing would be good for him and keep him right. In the plough he was not distressed with overwork, as some of the papers would make you believe, and if I had another like him I would do exactly the same with him under similar circumstances.

At the end of 1919 I sent Master Robert to Mr. Anthony to be trained as a 'chaser. He was out daily with Troytown, who was been trained for and eventually won, the Grand National in 1920. In his work with Troytown I thought at the time that Master Robert was doing too much, and after events go to prove that I was right. When the Grand National was over and won Master Robert was returned to me as being no good. He was soured, and when he came back he refused to work in chains."

Robert eventually sold Master Robert to Mr. J. T. Elliott from Strabane for £50. Mr. Elliott kept him for about six weeks, and for a time, Master Robert was kept on the Elliot's land on the Urney Road. The early morning train was on its way from Strabane to Ballybofey passing over the metal single line bridge known as the Camel's Hump. This spooked a number of horses including Master Robert who started to run along side the steam engine. For close on two miles Master Robert stayed with the train jumping hedges and ditches along the way to the amazement of the trains passengers and staff. On coming to the pile bridge it changed course, jumped a crossing gate on to the railway line in front of the train, and jumped another gate on to the Urney road at the Flushtown Bridge.

Master Robert was then sold a number of times, first to Mr. Laverty from Dungannon, then to Mr. Pat Rogers of Ratoath who sold him on to Mr. H. J. Fordham from Hertfordshire. Master Robert was eventually sold on to Major Sidney Green and Lord Airlie. Master Robert did race in a number of meetings with varying degrees of success, but it was over two successful races at Liverpool (3rd and 1st) over the greater part of the Grand National course that convinced his owners to give him a shot at the big one.

The time leading up to the Grand National did not bode well for Master Robert, first he bruised his fore pedal bone, which is inside the hoof causing frequent lameness. Further problems with jockey selection arose when Peter Roberts declined the ride because of Master Robert's injury, and so it fell to a freelance jockey, Bob Trudgill, not a man usually in a position to choose his mounts. However, twenty-four hours before the big race Trudgill had a bad fall needing stitches, but against medical advice weighed out to partner Master Robert.

Interviewed after the race Bob Trudgill gave the following account of the race; "They went much too fast for me in the early part of the race; after covering two miles and a half I must have been a furlong behind the leaders. Master Robert was not jumping well either. Twice I was hanging round his neck owing to mistakes he made. I could not get him to measure his fences properly. He repeatedly reached too far, and got his hind legs hung up, so that for a long time I did not fancy my chance, but when we were well into the 'country' the second time those in front began to come back to me. I had my whip out a long way from home, and I kept pushing 'Robert' as hard as I could. My hopes began to rise after we had crossed Valentine's for the second time, for I was then close to the leaders. After landing on the racecourse I gained on Silvo, and when I passed him I knew he was beaten. I cannot describe the sensation I felt as I came to the last fence in front, but I kept going for all I was worth till I had passed the winning post".

Master Robert

It is believed Master Robert was retired immediately after the Grand National but it is not known whether this was out of gratitude to Master Robert or because of his injury. We will end the story going back to the birth of Master Robert and how he got his name. Robert Mc Kinlay's son, also Robert believed at the time the horse was named after himself, a claim backed up by the fact that Dodds next foal by Moorside II, went by the name Master Alec, after the breeders younger son Alexander.

ROGANS of Glentown, Urney

By Dr. Phil Mowat

Exhaustive research by American scholars into Hugh Rogan and his family has generally assumed that his place of origin and that of his wife were undisputed and unconnected with Urney Parish.

From Rogan himself, who believed he was from Donegal, either Raphoe or Dunlewey appeared to be the only available options. As for his wife Ann Nancy, her birthplace was always accepted as Lisduff near Benburb in East Tyrone, as it was the only Tyrone Lisduff in the official surveys of the 19th century.

Hugh Rogan and his wife had inadvertently obscured their true place of birth for almost two centuries. In Hugh's case it was by placing himself in the wrong county and in Ann Nancy's case it was the ambiguity of the spelling in English of an Irish placename.

Nevertheless, the story of Hugh Rogan in America had been explored by a number of historians and much became known about him and his family. It was known that he was born in 'Glentourne' in Co Donegal and that Ann Duffy, aka Nancy, (his wife) was born in Lisduff, and was known as the 'fair maid of Omey' [Omagh]

When Hugh first went from Ireland to America in 1775 with his brother-in-law Daniel Carlin, to find available land on which to settle, they left behind teenage wives and in Rogan's case his firstborn, aged 6 months. As trained weavers, Rogan and Carlin brought linen they had woven to sell to cover the cost of their return journeys and their initial destination was south Virginia, where Daniel Carlin's brother owned/worked in a frontier shop.

For a variety of reasons, almost twenty two adventurous years passed before Rogan returned to collect his family, but from where? What can be abstracted from the American research is a body of circumstantial evidence that points to the most likely place of origin of both Hugh Rogan and his wife as two townlands in Urney Parish.

Hugh Rogan's story

Hugh Rogan was born on September 15th 1747. He was 28 years old and probably a very experienced weaver, able to generate a relatively good living, when he left for America in the Spring of 1775, following a sustained downturn in the profitability of the linen industry. He left behind Ann 'Nancy' [Duffy] Rogan, his wife, aged 18, and son Bernard, six months old.

The suggestion that he had more disposable income than most is based on his plan to undertake at least three journeys across the Atlantic, when many emigrants couldn't afford even one. Rogan's scouting mission to America to secure land was to be followed by a return to Ireland and a return journey to America with his family. For many previous emigrants, indenture [bartering future years of their labour in exchange for their new employer paying the cost of their passage] had been the only way of escaping poverty at home.

Years later in America, where Hugh Rogan had said he was from was written down and subsequently interpreted as 'Glentourne' Co Donegal. 'Glentourne' doesn't exist, but some researchers favoured Glenthorn, recorded as Glentornan near Dunlewey, as the closest match. The written record could be interpreted as 'Glentowne' and there was one such named townland in Donegal, near Raphoe.[Glentown]However, good contemporary records for Glentown show no Rogan or Duffy connection at the time he left Ireland or when he returned. Similarly, Glentornan has no contemporary record of Rogan or any related connections, despite a good oral history in this area.

If Rogan's townland could not be found in Donegal, it was necessary to look farther afield, particularly to adjoining counties.Rogan would not have been the first to have made a mistake about the county of his birth. In America in 1792, an immigrant called Calhoun from Crosh, near Newtownstewart told census recorders that he was from the Parish of Ardstraw, Co. Donegal!

At this time maps of some Parishes and demesnes existed, but county boundaries were as yet uncharted.The Tyrone/Donegal boundary was not to be mapped until Rogan had finally emigrated, the survey begun by McCrea in 1793 but engraved and printed only in 1807.

With the centre of the Parish of Urney lying in Donegal and Glentown's sloping fields taking in a panoramic view of that County, it would have been a natural mistake. When Hugh Rogan left Ireland for America in 1775, he was not expecting the outbreak of the American War of Independence which would close down his avenue of return to Ireland for some time.

Many years later, in 1845, a close friend of Hugh Rogan, General William Hall, recounted that Carlin and Rogan had first come to Surry County, North Carolina ("he came to Daniel Carland's in Surry County and lived there from 1775 to the fall of 1779 "

This implied that Carlin had acquired his own frontier land very soon after arrival in 1775, and it appears that indeed he had, along the disputed boundary between North Carolina and Virginia. The land was not in Surry County Virginia, however, but at Lambsburg on the Fincastle County Virginia side of the border.

From 1779 to 1780, after living for three years at Lambsburg with his brother-in-law, during which time he is believed to have fought in Daniel Carlin's company of the Virginia line regiment in the War of Independence, Rogan obtained work guarding the team of surveyors tasked with mapping the disputed North Carolina/Virginia State boundary.

After this, he joined land-speculator Colonel John Donelson's party in an rafting expedition westward down the Cumberland river to discover new lands suitable for settlement. Having survived Indian attacks, an outbreak of smallpox and the perils of a difficult white-water river descent, in 1780 he established a claim on a 640 acre tract of land in what is now Nashville, Tennessee and together with other first generation settlers in middle Tennessee, signed the Cumberland Compact to affirm their land rights.

Having land at his disposal as a negotiable asset, Rogan could now raise the funds to travel back to Ireland. He headed for home to retrieve his family in the spring of 1784, nine years after last seeing them. Four hundred miles into his journey, he stopped off at his brother-in –law's home at Lambsburg , by now incorporated into Carroll County.

Here, he was told by Carlin that the wife he was returning to had remarried, believing him to be dead. Other stories suggest Hugh Rogan was intercepted by a stranger bearing a letter from Ireland containing the same message. The stranger was allegedly paid by Daniel Carlin to deliver a forged message so that Hugh Rogan and Ann Nancy would never again meet.

The purpose, allegedly, was to prevent Hugh Rogan returning to Ireland with the news that Daniel Carlin had married a second wife in America and was himself a bigamist. After hearing the story of Ann Nancy's alleged re-marriage, Hugh returned to Sumner County, Tennessee in the autumn of 1785 where he settled at Bledsoe's fort on the Cumberland river.

His renowned exploits and his bravery were well documented as he repelled many brutal Indian onslaughts on the station's scattered population over the next ten years, throughout the course of the Cherokee War. It was only in 1795 that Rogan finally found out that his wife had remained faithful to him throughout all the years they had been apart and still awaited his return, twenty years on. With the Indian wars almost at an end, Rogan went to Ireland to collect his family in 1796 and returned to America with his wife and 22 year old son Bernard, on August 15th 1797. They travelled from the nearby port Londonderry to New Castle on the Delaware. In the following year, his second son, Francis, was born at Sumner County, Tennessee. Hugh was 51 and Ann Nancy 41 years old.

Hugh Rogan's house built c1798, Tennessee.

Ann 'Nancy' Rogan's story

According to Hugh Rogan, Ann and their infant son Bernard had been left in Co Tyrone, clearly within a stable family environment over the period of their long separation from Hugh. The family had ensured that Bernard obtained sound basic education.

According to the Rogan family bible, Ann Duffy was born on 17th March 1757 in Lisduff , Co Tyrone.For many years, this was assumed to be in the only officially recorded townland of that name in Tyrone, near Benburb. This was about as far away from Donegal as is possible in Tyrone. Such a distance would have made courtship problematic for Hugh and Ann Nancy!

The place names, Lisduff, and Lisdoo were interchangeable, as both mean 'black fort' in Irish. One 19th century County record refers to construction of an arch on the Castlefin to Newtownstewart road between Graffy and Lisduff, which could only be Lisdoo townland in Urney Parish.

Lisdoo is a short walk from Glentown, so Hugh, in common with the vast majority of people in Ireland at this time, married someone from within his own Parish.The name Duffy has long been associated with Lisdoo in Urney and it is probable that Ann Nancy and her son stayed with her family in the townland of her birth whilst Hugh was in America.

There were Duffy holdings in Lisdoo in 1803, John and Owen Duffy in one and Charles Duffy in another, contemporary with Ann Nancy's departure for Tennessee in 1797.By the time, of her death on 13th February 1839, several generations of her extended (Duffy) family had followed Ann Nancy to Tennessee from this part of Ireland.

Alternatively, around the time Hugh returned to retrieve his family, there were at least two Rogans living in the Parish of Urney, Daniel and John. It is possible that either of them, if kin to Hugh, could have provided a 'temporary' home for Hugh's young family.

Throughout her life, Ann Nancy had remained a devout Catholic and for nearly a half-century, it is reputed that her cottage kitchen in middle Tennessee remained the only place of Catholic worship in the vast region until Gallatin chapel was built in 1843.

Bernard Rogan's story

Born in Tyrone on the 12th of December 1774, Bernard, son of Hugh and Ann Nancy Rogan, was the oldest citizen of Sumner County Tennessee at his death in 1873, aged 98 years and 25 days.

His obituary (in 'The Tennessean', 1873) cited his experience in a company of United Irishmen, commanded by one Capt Murtaugh O'Flaherty. It was this reference which offered the strongest clue to Hugh's birthplace. The units of United Irishmen usually formed from an inter-related local population into 'societies' of 18 persons. Normally, 3 grouped societies elected a Captain.

Bernard's teenage years in the United Irishmen provided a firm pointer to where he and his mother were living while Hugh was in America. His Captain was most probably Murty Lafforty of Gortkilly in the Co. Donegal part of Urney Parish . Lafforty was a relatively prosperous tenant farmer whose 'home' farm faced east, overlooking nearby Lisduff and Glentown, but who had several other farms of land scattered throughout the Parish .

Shortly after his arrival in America, Bernard left the father he had never really known and went to the Spanish Territory, now Missouri. By 1803, he was exercising the legal powers and authority of an Alcalde [Governor/Administrator] in the area of modern-day Austin, Texas by virtue of being born an Irish Catholic.

The Spaniards believed that an English-speaker with his background would best serve their interests in administering an ever - growing English- speaking settler population.

In later years he served under General Howard against the Indians in 1813 (in what is now the State of Illinois) and made a lifelong friend of Major Nathan Boone, youngest son of the famous frontiersman Daniel Boone.

He finally retired to brother Francis's new Plantation house at Bledsoe's Creek in 1821 and fifty years later was presented with regalia by the 'Hibernian Society' of Nashville as the last survivor of the 'United Irishmen of 1798'

American-born Francis Rogan's story will be told when his original Tennessee Plantation home, which was recorded, dismantled and transported brick by individually-numbered brick, is rebuilt and opened at the Ulster American Folk Park in the summer of 2011. [Francis became a major plantation owner, owning 71 slaves at the outbreak of the American Civil war.]

The extraordinary exploits of this pioneer family from Urney Parish, Co.Tyrone, will again be recounted around the hearth of their original home, just as their descendants might have done over the past centuries.

Castlefinn G.A.A.

By Samuel Gallagher and Mary Mc Connell

A G.A.A. Club was founded in Castlefinn in 1918 under the name Con Culberts. Two of the Founder members were M. O'Doherty and J.O. Flaherty, Carrick. There were two teams in Castlefinn for the Strabane and district league of 1922, St Mary's and Emmet's. It is not known which team emerged to represent East Donegal in the senior championship. It is possible that they coalesced for the championship. Castlefinn emerged triumphant in the final by three points against Glenties for Castlefinn's first and only senior championship.

Some of the players at that time where
Jimmy Doherty, John Noonan, Hugh John Reilly, Eddie Geary, John Mc Glinchey, Thomas – Joseph Carlin, Jimmy Dooher, Thomas Dooher, George Patrick Dooher, George Dooher, Mick Dooher, Patrick Dooher, Rev. Willie Mortland, Jonny Patton.

The Club continued to field at Snr. level and in 1926 they finished in the runners up spot in the County League Competitions. By 1927 Castlefinn still had the two football teams, however Emmets failed to play any of their games. St Mary's went on to finish joint third in the league with a very memorable last game against Carrigans. "It was 'one of the finest games ever witnessed at Sessiagh park' and Castlefinn won it by 4-4 to 2-3. Woods (Castlefinn) and Mc Goldrick exchanged early points. Higgins (Castlefinn) and Harry Francis then exchanged goals. A point put Carrigans 1-2 to 1-1 ahead at half time. Castlefinn took command against the hill. Kelly pointed to equalise. W.J. Bonner's goal gives Castlefinn the lead, but Mc Nulty's goal levelled it once more. Maxwell (Castlefinn) and Mc Nulty exchanged points – 2-3 each. But two Woods' goals and a Kelly point secured victory for St Mary's Castlefinn." (The story of the Donegal Senior Football Championship 1919-2001, Seán O' Gallchóir.)

In 1930 they again finished in the runners up spot in the County League Competition and they were Jnr. Championship Runners Up in 1939 when they lost to Cloughaneely in Falcarragh. They won the Jnr. Championship in 1945 when they defeated Corlea in Donegal Town.

Wearing Amber and Black the team that day was:
Tommy McAleer, Mannie Catterson, Packie Quinn, Jeordie Crawford, Wm. Tinney, Jim Quinn, Jimmy Clarke, Joe Ruse, Sean Donnelly, Hugo Devine, Solly McGhee, Paddy McNulty (Capt), Joe McBride, Eddie Catterson, Jim McGhee.

Subs – E. McCrossan;   Mgr. - Dr. McMenamin

The Club was out of action between 1947 and 1950. With no permanent field they played at Jack Porter's field known as The Rushey Field. They were Jnr. Champions again in 1951, defeating St. Nauls (Inver) in Glenties wearing Blue jerseys with white collars and cuffs.

Robert Emmets 1951 Junior Champions.
Back row – Jim Druce, Sean Donnelly, Paddy Brennan, Danny Mc Monagle, Joe Mc Bride, Pat Mc Bride, Hugo Devine, Packie Quinn.
Front Row – Paddy Mc Nulty, Barney Tinney, Willie Edwards, Solly Mc Ghee, Dan Brolly, Sean Kelly Pat O' Shea, Dan Derry.

They again reached the Jnr. Final in 1953 but this Final was not played until 1954 because of some dispute over the Referee, which caused the Inver team to walk off the field. When it was finally played in 1954 in Barnesmore, they were again crowned Jnr. Champions.

Wearing Blue jerseys with white collars and cuffs the team was:
Barney Tinney, Wm. Edwards, Paddy Brennan, Kevin Kelly, Raymond Bryson, Sean McGinley (Cust), Jas Bryson, Paddy McBride, Solly McGhee, Hugo Devine, Paddy McNulty, Sean O'Callaghan (Cust), Dessie Bryson, Sean Kelly, Eamonn Catterson, Charley McGroarty.

The Club reached the County Minor Championship Final in 1954 but suffered defeat at the hands of Ardara. In 1955 Eamon Catterson proposed changing the name of the club from St. Mary's to Robert Emmets. This proposal was carried and the job of rebuilding the club began. A team was gathered up to replace Urney in "An Tostal" tournament in Ballybofey. They managed to win the tournament beating both Mc Cools and St. Eunan's in the process.

So in 1956 a mood of optimism prevailed within the club. The team was managed by Roger Eames, a potato Inspector from Leitrim, who had represented his county as far away as the polo grounds in New York. A rigorous training campaign was initiated with training three nights weekly. Jim Druce and Pat Brennan took charge of training in the hall. Road running, supervised by Jim Druce on a bicycle, was also part of the training programme. Their dedication was evident, which some players can remember, as they trained with Aussie Bryson at 6a.m. on a Sunday morning. The painstaking training regime paid off as the team progressed through the Eastern Divisional Championship. The biggest stumbling block for the team at this time was always Lifford, who were made up of Customs men, Garda and locals, who were always a very strong side.

After winning through in East Donegal, they qualified to play Ardara in the county semi final in Letterkenny. After a tough game the team progressed to the county final and a tough encounter with Bundoran. Bundoran fielded a young side comprising players such as Mickey Mcloone, Brian McEniff, Declan O Carroll, Peter Quinn, Jackie McDermott and the Fitzgerald brothers.

A fine game ensued with Emmets getting the upper hand. Highlights from that game were a solid performance from the half back line of Bryson, Willie Edwards and McGroarty, a solid midfield performance by Eamon Catterson and a forward line, all of whom got on the score sheet. Honour too goes to Barney Tinney who saved a penalty just when it looked as if Bundoran may have gained the upper hand. A final score of 2-6 to Emmets and 1-4 to Bundoran saw the first half of a double complete!!!

The league campaign was a successful one which again saw them reach the final and again the opponents were Bundoran. Patsy Carlin, club secretary, proposed that the final be played in Ballyshannon. He did this because he felt that the experience of the side had been limited to playing in the East. His proposal was agreed to and both sides met in Ballyshannon. Emmets won the game by a score line of 1-8 to 0-2. When County Board official Sean Slevin went to present the cup he found he couldn't. Apparently the Bundoran goalkeeper named McNulty was a little upset at having been beaten by Castlefinn yet again and he decided to abscond with the cup! However one of the Fitzgerald brothers went after him, retrieved the cup and all was well. Following their double success of 1956, they again became League Champions in 1958 when they defeated Bundoran in Donegal Town, but they had to wait until 1961 for their next Jnr. Championship success, which they also doubled up with League success. In the Jnr. Championship Final, which was played in Letterkenny, they were victorious over Cresslough. In 1964 they were back in a Jnr. Championship Final but lost to Glenties. There then followed a period of inactivity from 1964 until 1968.

The formation of the present club as we now know it took place on the 23rd February 1968 when following a meeting, Castlefinn Emmetts were formed and the following officers were elected:

Pres.	Rev. Fr. McSorley
Chair.	Aussie Bryson
V. Chair.	Willie Gallagher
Sec.	Sgt. McBride
Ass. Sec.	Jim Druce
Treas,	John Boyce
Comm.	Billy Patton, Sean Kelly, Pat McBreen, Patsy McCormick, Patsy McMenamin, Terence McLaughlin, Raymond Bryson, Sam Gallagher, Sean Donnolly and P.H. Carlin, who after 20 years service as Treasurer, stepped aside due to work commitments

That year the club won the Fr. Bradley cup defeating Aghyaran 1-9 to 0-4 in the Final.

In 1970 Robert Emmets won the U16 County Championship.

The team that day was:
Coleman McGhee, Paul McNulty, Hugh McMenamin, John Mulloy, Anthony Catterson, Patrick Murray, Declan McConnell, Louis Walsh, John Coyle, Johnny Curran (Capt), Gabrial Gordon, Brian Boyle, Paul McGhee, Sean Hunter, Brian Doherty, Leo Elliott, Tony Elliott, John McGarrigle, Paul McMenamin, John Gordon, Noel Murray, Larry Doherty.

Success again came in 1975 when we won the U14 County Championships.
We were also crowned Div 2 League Champions in 1975.
1975 also saw the Club reach the County U21 Final where we played McCools in McCool Park. We were defeated in this game and although it was little consolation for the club and the team, it was said that this was one of the best games of football played at the venue for many years.

The team that day was:
Cathal Wright, Tony Elliott, Christy Murray, Brian Harvey, Gabrial Gordon, Johnny Curran, Sandy Harper (R.I.P), Louis Walsh, Leo Elliott, Paul McGhee, Same McGirr, John Gordon, Coleman McGhee, Peter O'Connor.

Subs used: Noel Murray, Larry Doherty

Ref. T. McBrearty (St. Nauls).

In 1981, it was our U12 team's turn to taste success when they became County Champions defeating Aodh Ruadh Beal Atha Seanaidh. The Club won two All Ireland in the 1980's but not on the field. It was in the Jnr. Scor Instrumental Music Section when the talented Harper Family from Dungorman became All Ireland Champions in 1980 and 1982.

In the midst of the jubilations in 1980 and 1982, the club experienced one of its darkest days when following a tragic road traffic accident Sandy Harper, one the Club's and County's most promising young footballers passed away. The Club hosted The Sandy Harper Memorial Tournament for the following 25 years and now Sandy's memory is honoured with the County Div 1 B winners receiving the Prestigious Sandy Harper Memorial Cup.

After a lapse of 22 years, 1986 saw Robert Emmetts back in a County Jnr. Championship Final, but they suffered defeat at the hands of Naomh Brid. However, success again came to the Club in 1987 when we were crowned Jnr. Champions defeating Four Masters. We again suffered defeat in the 1995 and 2001 Finals at the hands of Convoy and Urris respectively before tasting success in 2002 when we again lifted the Jnr. Championship, defeating Naomh Brid in the Final.

In 2004, tragedy again struck the Club when Shaun T. Carlin lost his life following an unfortunate incident in Letterkenny. Shaun T. was a great clubman and a talented and dedicated footballer. The Club have named their stand after Shaun T. and ran a very popular Shaun T. Carlin Memorial Tournament each year until 2010.

In 2008 we won Div 4 of the League and reached the Jnr. County Final.

Pairc Eimeid, is the home of Roibeaird Eimeid, with an excellent pitch, covered stand, dressing rooms, gym and kitchen facilities. We are very proud of our facilities and the fact that the County Snr. Team use these facilities as their training headquarters. The present Club colours are Navy Blue/Sky Blue.

The Club have supplied the county with players at different levels through its existence. The following at Snr. level: M. O'Flaherty (1920), E. Boyle (1921), J. Quinn (1936/37/38), P. Quinn (1939/40), S. Donnelly (1949), with the most notable in recent times being Andy Curran (1968-1976), Sandy Harper (1977-1980),Eugene Mc Menamin in the victorious Vocational school team of 1985, Martin Mc Menamin in 1995 and Marcus Curran in 2002. In 1954 the County contested the All Ireland Jnr. Final in Croke Park against Kerry. The talented Raymond Bryson who lined out at right corner back represented Castlefinn.

We have also supplied the County with County Officers, EG. Minor Board Chairman – Gabrial Gordon, Snr. Board Secretary – Seamus O'Donnell who has held the post as County Sec. County P.R.O. and is currently the County Treasurer, Dominic McGlinchey who managed the County Snr. Ladies Team.

It is now over 90 years since the formation of the G.A.A. in Castlefinn and we have been very fortunate to have had genuine and dedicated Gaels to maintain and hand on the ideals and the traditions of Cumann Luth Chleas Gael to each generation and this responsibility now rests on the present Club to ensure that we do not fail in our duty to maintain, develop and promote the proud traditions of Cumann Luth Chleas Gael in this area under the auspices of Fo-Chumann Roibeard Eimiid,

Robert Emmets U14 girls

Castlefinn Celtic

By Eunan O Brien

The summer of 1982 saw the emergence of Castlefin Celtic on the Donegal soccer map. The Club played in the old Letterkenny based "Hospital League" for the first six years before entering the Donegal League in 1988. In that inaugural season the Division 3 title was secured but undoubtedly the highlight of the year was the winning of the Donegal Area Final of the FAI Junior Cup. Four victories over teams from higher divisions qualified us for the final against the then Junior Soccer "Kingpins" Ardara Town. Against all odds we won the final and qualified for the national stages of the cup. Waterford Bohemians made the long trip north for the last sixteen fixture of the national competition and despite a marvellous performance we lost 3–1 out in Tommy Moss' field in Doneyloop to a stronger and more experienced side. What a first season!

Our progress continued in 89/90 when we captured the Division 2 title and gained promotion to the top tier of Donegal Junior Football. The 1990/91 season saw us consolidate our position in Division 1.

Sadly, 1991 will be remembered for the sudden death of Damien Brolly, one of our most promising footballers. The Damien Brolly Memorial Cup was run for ten years in his memory. 91/92 was also the inaugural season of the Premier Division of the Donegal League. Only a lapse in our final two league games prevented us from winning the title, eventually finishing up third. This was to be our highest finish in the Donegal League. A memorable FAI Junior cup game was played in Drumdoit where the school is now built. Our old foes Lifford Celtic edged us in a typical local derby thanks to the heroics of one Shay Given. It was later in this cup run that Shay was spotted and that ultimately led to his cross channel career.

Shay Given (on ground) playing for Lifford Celtic against Castlefin Celtic in Drumdoit in the 1991/1992 season.

Castlefin Celtic 1991/1992 Sunday Team pictured in the grounds of Doneyloop Community Centre prior to a match in Drumdoit

Our fortunes have fluctuated since those early years with the club experiencing both relegations and promotions. The capture of the Division 1 title in 96/97 and the Donegal Saturday League Division 2 title in 01/02 were undoubtedly high points. In 2000 the Sunday team again qualified for the national stages of the FAI Junior Cup, losing out in Jonstown, Co. Kilkenny to Spa Utd.

In May 2004 we again lost one of our most talented footballers following the tragic death of Sean T. Carlin. As with Damien his death left a huge void in our club.

Our senior teams continue to challenge for honours in Division 1 of the Donegal Sunday League and Division 2 of the Donegal Saturday League with both teams comprised almost entirely of players from the Urney and Castlefin Parish.

In recent times a lot of resources have been put into our underage teams. Numerous club personnel have now completed FAI approved Coaching Courses. The benefit of this approach has become evident with success on the playing field and a lot more of our players being recognised at a higher level. The club has captured numerous Lifford & District and East Donegal Underage Titles. Undoubtedly our biggest achievement to date has been the winning of the Donegal under 16 Champions League Title in 08/09. We so nearly emulated that success last season when our Under 12's lost out narrowly in their county final.

Many of our young players have played on both East Donegal and Donegal underage teams with the club being particularly well represented on Donegal Kennedy Cup teams in 2006 and 2007. Three players who have come up through our ranks namely Barry Tourish, Ciaran Gallagher and Tanya Kennedy have gone on to gain full International caps. Indeed Barry, Ciaran, Aaron O Hagan and Raymond Foy have all gone on to play for the Finn Harps first team. Our under age system continues to flourish with our teams competing against the best in Grade A competitions. Some players move on to a higher level but the vast majority that come up through the under age ranks go on to play for our senior teams.

While making good progress on the pitch, significant advances have also been made in the ground development area. In 1992 a six acre site was purchased in Ballybun and by the summer of 1995 two playing pitches had been developed. The construction of our clubrooms was completed in 2002. An all weather pitch has been added, with one of our pitches now fully floodlit for training purposes. In the region of €200,000 has been spent on the development with approximately one third grant aided. The balance was raised through various fund raising schemes.

May 18th, 2003 was an important date in the Club's calendar with Shay Given performing the official opening of our facilities in Ballybun. Sadly one of the principle organisers of that day has since passed away. John White was a pivotal member of our club since its formation. His enthusiasm and will to succeed was an inspiration to us all.

The current Club Committee is as follows:

Chairman:	Fintan O Hagan
Vice Chairman:	Damien Mc Aneney
Secretary:	Lana Sweeney
Assistant Secretary:	Damien Mc Glinchey
Treasurer:	Adrian Gallagher
Assistant Treasurer:	Eunan O Brien
PRO:	Anthony Sweeney
Other Committee Members:	Anthony White, Kevin White, Damien Doherty, Ciaran Brennan and Darragh Crossan.

Senior Team Managers:	Eunan O Brien and Pat Molloy
Reserve Team Managers:	Kevin White and Mervin Stewart
Under 8 Team Managers:	Michael Dunnion and Fintan O Hagan
Under 10 Team Managers:	Damien Mc Glinchey and Adrian Gallagher
Under 12 Team Managers:	Fintan O Hagan and Cormac O Brien
Under 14 Team Managers:	Gerard Catterson and Darren Catterson
Groundsman:	Joe Dunnion

Urney St Columba's

By Pat Holland

The current Urney St Columba's has been in continuous existence since 1945. There have been clubs in the village from 1903. (Clady Rory Óg and 1921-1922 William Pearses).Anecdotal evidence has it that Gaelic games were played at Skelpy prior to 1900 but there is no concrete evidence of this.

Clady Rory Óg played Newtonstewart in 1903 at Newtonstewart. After discussion of the rules with Newtonstewart a game took place and the Rory Óg lost by 3 -00 to 1 - 00 The Rory Ógs won the return fixture.
 In the 1907 Tyrone Championship Cup Strabane Lamh Dherg drew Clady Rory Óg and advanced to the next round. It was at this time that Rory Óg disappeared from the scene. At the 1908 County Convention Rory Óg were represented by J.P. Lennon.

In December 1919 Colemans of Omagh travelled to Clady for a challenge game and a second game took place in Omagh at Lisnamallard Holm on 11 January 1920. Clady were described as "one of the best Gaelic teams in Donegal."In 1921 the Derry v Donegal Ulster Seniors football Championship was played at the Bog Road, Strabane. Derry won by 2 - 01 to 00 - 03 but note that the Donegal Scores came from two Clady players Elliot and Ó Flaherty, while other unfamiliar Clubs represented on the Donegal lineout were Rabstown (Ponsenby) and Bellalt (Maxwell).

On 24th July 1921 Clady travelled to Glenties so that the newly founded Glenties GAA team could learn some of the finer points of the game with the return fixture on 7th August 1921 which Glenties won by two points. A league was set up to cater for the Gaels of the North West Tyrone and South East Donegal; meetings took place in Barrack Street, while Leckpatrick Curate Fr Thomas Bradley was to the forefront of GAA activity in the area. The league included teams from Clady (William Pearses) and Clady (Fine Gael) and also included teams from Sion Mills (Owen Roes) Castlefin (St Marys). The league was short lived and ceased on 21st May 1922 due to difficulties in travelling.

The West Tyrone Board of the Tyrone GAA was set up in 1931 with twenty eight clubs registered by the 6th January 1932 with teams from Sion Mills and Clady included. In late 1932 a North Tyrone Board established a junior league to include a team from Clady. A Newspaper report Derry Journal 25th November 1932 held from that time stated "after a lapse of ten years a Gaelic football team has been formed in Clady." It contains family names that still appear on team selects to-day. Haughey – Kane – Nelis – McNulty –Langan. Frank Canning refereed the game.

At this time 1933, there was a Gaelic revival in Clady and the Ulster Herald wrote "A great change has taken place in the quiet little village of Clady with its long rows of neat well kept cottages situated by the pleasant banks of the River Finn." A Gaelic revival has come to stay; Irish dancing has taken its rightful place in the people's innocent pastimes.

Urney consisting of players from Melmount, Sion Mills and Clady met Killyclogher in the Senior Championship at Clady. The Ulster Herald reported "it would be well to mention the position of the pitch which is unique in as much as it's bordered on two sides by the Free State." So it would be as well to park all cars belonging to the six counties in the village or vicinity. Urney lost on a score of 2 - 04 to 2 - 05."

Football went well in 1934 and the names of Frank Haughey and Mick Kane appear to the fore in match reports. On 20th October 1934 Clady defeated Grange to win the North Tyrone Junior Championship having already won the league. They played Greencastle in 1935 in the County Semi-final and won 3 - 00 to 0 - 02.The final was played in Dregish on 16 February 1935 against Moortown with Urney taking the title on a score of 2 - 02 to 0 – 03. Alas, success was short lived as Moortown protested as to the composition to the Clady team deemed to have included a number of players from East Donegal. The game was lost in the Boardroom and it would take another fifty-six years before Urney would won the Junior Championship in 1990 when they beat Aghaloo on score of 2 - 08 to 0 - 07.

At this point Clady withdrew from all activities and took no part in GAA affairs for ten years. This takes us up to the formation our current club Urney St Columba's.

THE REBIRTH OF THE GAA

From 1936 to 1944 one can only assume that soccer took over again. There is no known reason why it took so long to be reformed. At this time there was opposition to setting up of a Gaelic team in Clady and after much argument, debate and physical disputes finally all things came to a head. A meeting was held in Billy Mc Gees house but the decision could not be resolved so a secret ballot took place to see whether it be Gaelic or soccer football. So on Good Friday night the votes were cast and counted by Eddie Lafferty (a family name that with others has been an ever present). This is where it becomes clouded, both sides believed they had won before the vote was announced, majority of one for Gaelic football.

As they prepared for a return to Gaelic football there were three football teams operating in the area. St Bridget's which consisted of mainly young players, Oliver Plunketts where made up of the older generation and a third team organised by Dr Hagan. A match was arranged to see who was the better side St Bridget's or St Plunketts. St Bridget's were to the fore when the ball was mysterious punctured so the problem was not resolved. Towards the end of 1944 the Finn Valley league was resurrected.

The St Bridget's represented the village in 1945 but lost to Gortin after a replay thus ending St Bridget's journey in Tyrone. However at the 1946 Tyrone convention St Bridget's and the Plunketts were represented by three delegates each. However the chairman Fr Kirk advised that both sets of delegates should return home and resolve the problem among themselves. Fr Mc Hugh the Parish Priest summoned representatives of both Clubs to meet with him. He advised if they remain divided then they were going nowhere. He amalgamated the three teams and called the new team Urney St Columba's. It took some time before the Bridget's and Plunketts accepted his decision.

URNEY ST COLUMBAS took the pitch in 1946 and have remained in existence henceforth. There are many stories told and it is difficult to decide what is factual and what is fiction. Sometime later it was rumoured that Fr Mc Hugh put a curse on the teams present at the meeting that neither would ever win a championship. This hung over the club for years resulting in teams believing they couldn't win a championship at adult level. It took the team of 1990 to break the "curse" by winning the Junior Championship at the third attempt. They lost to Pomeroy in 1984 (Centenary Year) and to Drumquin in 1987.

There is limited evidence of how Urney performed in the years 1945-46 but at county level Urney made an impact with Billy Melly and Robert Mc Nulty becoming part of the Tyrone minor panel Robert played right through to the defeat by Dublin in the All Ireland semi final. Robert played at corner back and Billy played against Antrim but was dropped for the semi final against Derry. Robert played in the 1947 Minor team at full back and went on to claim Ulster and All Ireland minor medals.

Urney had played in the Junior League but come 1947, the County Board promoted them to the senior ranks where they played in the West Tyrone League against Gortin, Dromore, Newtonstewart, Strabane and Omagh. Urney were paired against Strabane in the senior football Championships, Strabane had won the 1945 senior title where four Urney men had starred –Hughie Kelly, Francie Houston, Jimmy Hamilton and Josel Mc Nulty.

Urney lost their first senior game to Gortin 0 - 09 to 0 - 05 in treacherous conditions. It was at this time that Urney sought permission for the Fr Bradley Cup to be played in Donegal!!! Reports indicate Urney beat Strabane 0 - 14 to 0 – 08 in what was described as a surprise and well merited win. Controversy raised its head again about an over age player in the minor football championship v Ballygawley when Ballygawley raised questions regarding one of the Urney players, his autograph was sought but he refused. Ballygawley protested but lost because they sought his autograph after the game.

In a report of the 1948 Annual General Meeting The Ulster Herald congratulated the newly elected committee for appealing to the club to promote hurling. Urney were the only club to mention hurling at that time. In March of 1949 the" Local Derby" between Strabane and Urney was played, again before a large crowd. Urney were worthy winners of an exciting game on the score of 3 – 02 to 0 – 04. The second leg took place a week later with Urney drawing away in the second half on a score of 1 – 10 to 0 – 02. By mid season Urney were unbeaten when they met Gortin who had won the league the season before. This was a titanic struggle played at a fast pace and providing a clean game with Gortin winning on a score of 1 – 06 to 1 – 03. Gortin refused to travel for the second game but following a board meeting agreed to do so. Following a sharp game with some spectator input Urney ran out winners on a score of 2 – 06 to 0 – 05.

Trouble was never too far away and in early 1950's Urney was alleged to have played five unregistered players. It transpired that the delegates walked out of the meeting and with Strabane showing a lack of interest, the North Tyrone Board looked to be failing. A special investigation committee was set up to investigate the situation. They suspended the three Urney delegates for twelve months. The club formed a new committee and returned to the league. The North Tyrone Board was reformed in 1951.

The Mc Elduff Cup was competed for the first time and Urney lost to Carrickmore on a score of 1 – 08 to 1 – 04. In August of that year a juvenile game between Ballybofey St Malachey's and Urney took place with a band parade from the village to the pitch. The game ended in a draw. This game drew much praise from the press for its skills. Urney lost in the St Enda's Cup to Omagh at the semi final stage.

In 1952 details are limited with Urney losing to Omagh in the St Enda's Cup. The Davis Cup for 1953 did not come to completion until the early part of 1954 when Urney and Dromore met in the semi final. After a poor first half Urney ran out easy winners by a score of 3 –0 8 to 1 – 03. In the final on the 6th February at Mourne Park in Strabane, Urney met Cappagh and when Cappagh fell away in the second half Urney won easily on a score of 2 –0 6 to 0 – 04. After this Urney returned to the West Tyrone League and beat Trillick in the first round of the Championship with a score of 3 – 08 to 0 – 05. Urney fell at the quarter finals of the Championships when Dungannon won on a score of 1 –0 8 to 2 – 02. Urney were suspended for two years for incidents after the game but won their appeal to Ulster Council with the suspension been reduced to six months.

Urney qualified for the West Tyrone final against Carrickmore when controversy clouded the game. Carrickmore won on a score of 1 – 08 to 2 – 04. However everyone, bar the Carrickmore team and supporters were of the opinion that a Carrickmore shot had gone over the bar rather than under it, which would have meant Urney should have won by one point. Urney appealed claiming that one of the Carrickmore players was a US. airman. They lost at the West Tyrone Board but had the decision reversed at the Tyrone County Board hearing who ordered that the game be replayed. Urney won the replay when it took place in 1956 and thus lifted the 1955 title.

Again Urney lost in the County Championship in 1956 at the quarterfinal stage when they fell to Clonoe. Urney were matching Clonoe all over the pitch for the first fifteen minutes until a high ball deceived the goalkeeper and ended up in the back of the net. During the 1956 season club delegate Joe Hunter enquired when the 1955 St Enda's Cup was taking place as the Urney players wanted to know before going on their annual working term in Scotland. The game was finally played in September when Urney won by a score of 3 – 06 to 1 -04, Urney were superior in virtually every position.

Meanwhile Urney success continued when they defeated Newtownstewart 1-11 to 1-02 to retain the Davis Cup with Dermot Gallagher the star player. They defeated Letterkenny to win the inaugural Sean McCumhaill Memorial Cup. However as usual, Urney failed to progress in the County Championship losing to Ballygawley in the first round.

Urney in the 1950's

Again at the start of 1957, the dark clouds hung over the club as Urney met Carrickmore in the West Tyrone League Final losing by a point 2-06 to 1-08. After taking part in the Beragh tournament the Club was suspended for 12 months for playing two illegal players against Clogher. However this news was not supported by all other clubs within the County. Clubs felt that senior football in North Tyrone would cease if the club was suspended as they were the only strong club in the area and most clubs also thought the County Board's action was short-sited. It was also stated that most teams from Tyrone and Derry were competing in tournaments with illegally constituted teams. With all this support, Urney finally appealed to the Ulster Council stating that the Urney parish takes in Donegal and Tyrone areas.

The Ulster Council ruled in favour of Urney and reinstated the club. This also established Urney's right to play those players from the Donegal end of the parish – (this was reversed some years ago by the then Ulster Council and included many other clubs whose parish crosses intercounty boundaries). It should be noted that the Tyrone County Convention took place in Donegal (at Doneyloop Parochial Hall) on the 13th January 1991.

Urney won four of their first five matches and because of their style of play they received many invitations to tournaments in counties Derry, Tyrone and Donegal. The Letterkenny Tournament was top notch with Armagh Harps, Letterkenny, Omagh, Clontibert, Stranorlar, Coalisland, Keady and Urney. This reads almost as an Ulster Club Championship.

Urney had S. Bogle and S. McLaughlin on the Tyrone Minor Team while L. Strain had a seat on the bench. This gave Urney confidence that they would do well in the championship where the team was coached by Sean McCutcheon. During the year the team played twenty games winning 18 and losing 2. However, in the minor Championship they won the West Tyrone Final beating Ballygawley and went on to play Ardboe in the final. Urney created history when they defeated Ardboe on a score of 2-04 to 0-09 becoming the first Urney team to win a county title in September 1959.

Urney also qualified for the St. Enda Cup Final but the game was never played. Urney made inroads in the Senior Championship in 1961 beating Edendork by 0-11 to 0-05 to reach the semi final before throwing the game away having led by 8 points at half time against Moy. However, they made amends in the League winning their section and going on to defeat Newtownstewart in the final (McElduff Cup).

Even though Urney won the West Tyrone League in 1961, they had to meet Trillick in a playoff for a top 4 spot in the League. Both teams were furious especially Urney who had reached the semi-final the year before. Nevertheless Urney beat Trillick in the play off by 1-10 to 1-06. Urney proved their point when they went on to beat Moy in the quarter final by 2-09 to 1-03 and were the only West Tyrone club in the semi-finals. Unfortunately on the morning of the semi-final Eddie McCrory died and his two sons in law, Billy Melly and Eugene McNulty could not travel to the match. Bill Melly was the manager. Urney met disaster in the game when H. O'Kane was sent off within five minutes and then gave away an own goal. They were finally beaten 2-04 to 0-05.

In 1963 Urney led the table with 7 wins from 7 games but still conspired to lose the League to Carrickmore. At Convention in 1964 the Club were deemed to be in debt to the sum of £1 and 10 shillings. Nevertheless it was agreed that should they win the St. Enda Cup they should fill Flanagan's Bar. On the field of play Urney qualified for the Final of the Fr. Campbell Cup against Clonoe who were hot favourites. In one of the best games for many years Urney were victorious on a score of 1-08 to 0-10. After twelve games in the League, Urney led Carrickmore by one point but fell back after being deducted four points for unregistered players. Having qualified for another St.Enda's Cup final they failed miserably losing on a score of 1-00 to 3-03 with the goal coming from a penalty in the final minutes.

The mid sixties saw Urney as the Kingpins and crowd puller at Tournaments throughout Tyrone, Donegal, Derry and Fermanagh and with the occasional trip to Antrim. They won outright at these venues frequently and organisers "fixed" dream games here:- Urney v Ballygawley, Armagh Harps, Clontibert, McCumhaill, Omagh, Dromore – the list is endless, the gates were huge e.g. Armagh Harps v Urney at the Dromore Tournament - takings £240 at 2 shillings per head, i.e. at least 2,400 paying spectators. At today's rates this would be at least £10,000.

Urney continued to clean up in Club Tournaments in 1966 including the Omagh Tournament where they beat Dromore 5-12 to 1-07 in the semi-final and Omagh St. Enda's in the final on a score of 1-12 to 1-05. Shortly after, they won the Aghyaran Tournament. At the half way stage Urney led Omagh by 2 points in the league with 7 wins out of 7 games. By the end of the season, they won the League with 24 pts (2 losses) from Carrickmore on 19 points. To go with the League, Urney also beat Stewartstown in the final of the Fr.Campbell Cup for the second time in three years.

At the end of the year Urney had played 23 games, drawn 3 and lost 6 – one of which was because of the late arrival on the pitch.

In 1967 Urney defeated Omagh in the League and Moy in the Fr. Campbell Cup and Championship before disposing of Carrickmore in the Omagh Tournament. The successful team this year was the Juvenile Team who defeated Strabane in the North Tyrone Final by 0-12 to 1-03. This team included a number of players from the then other half of the parish Castlederg. Urney went onto lose the final to a very strong Coalisland team after a reply on a score of 2-03 to 1-03.

Urney found it difficult to remain outside the relegation zone in 1968 but were saved as the All County Leagues were set up with Urney being in Section B. Urney finished in a mid-table position that year. Urney continued to play in the "B" section in 1970 and the highlight was qualifying for a St.Enda's Cup Final against old rivals Carrickmore. This turned out to be a very intense game – "it was tough, uncompromising but fair brand of football" played by Urney. Jack Langan starred and scored 1-04. Urney had one player sent off but still won the game. Unfortunately Urney fell foul of the "top table" following a robust game against Clonoe at Cutt Park resulting in several players being suspended and the Club received a six months suspension.

By the start of 1973 Urney had been relegated to the Intermediate grade but because of the success of the Tyrone team, Urney were promoted back to senior grade because they topped an unfinished League table. They survived in Section B of the League with a mid table finish – one of 3 teams on 17 points. During 1974 it was decided that all clubs would play in an all county system resulted in Urney being placed in Div 2 for the 1975 season. Life in Div 2 got off to a bad start with the team losing their first three games and collecting 4 points from their eight games.

The club did not fair any better in 1976 losing out to Strabane in the Intermediate Championship and playing Strabane in a relegation play off in Div 3, which Urney won easily by 3-07 to 0-06.This reprieve was short-lived as Urney found themselves in the same position the following year after a perceived amalgamation between Urney and Strabane failed to materialise.

At the end of the season Urney and Omagh met in the last League game of the season, Urney needed two points to avoid a relegation playoff and Omagh needed two points to gain a play off for the title against Aghyaran. Urney lost to Omagh leaving them to play Edendork in a playoff but they were docked two points by the

Sylvester Kirk playing in Croke Park

County Board resulting in relegation to Div 4 by the end of 1977.

They survived in Div 4 in 1978 by finishing 5th out of 8 teams. At the end of this season it was decided to re-organise the leagues again on a 16 team structure of 3 sections for the year 1979. Urney again struggled to remain in the new Div 2 in 1979 going seven games without a victory. They were relegated at the end of the season to Div 3 (Jnr League) and it would take 10 years to get out of this position. The start of the '80's brought hope but no success. As usual the championship search was fruitless as they lost to Loughmacrory in the semi-final having defeated Greencastle in the first round on a score of 2-05 to 0-07. The League performance was poor finishing third from bottom. Again Urney was suspended for a year following incidents in a game against Loughmacrory. Urney was idle for the year of 1981.

As a result Urney needed to rise from the ashes again so a new committee was set up with Paul McNulty at the helm but the County Board called them to a meeting to decide whether or not they should be allowed back into football. Questions came thick and fast as Paul answered with the first thing came to mind. Emphasis was placed on a disciplinary committee within the club to which Paul indicated that they had set up. Paul indicated that they would have U21; Minor; U14 and U12 teams, when in fact they would be struggling to get one adult team out. After due deliberation by the County Disciplinary Committee they were advised that night that because they had so many teams available especially at youth level that they would be allowed to compete.

One result of this new committee that was so unusual is that Urney were awarded a prize of being the best disciplined team. Since then incidents have been few and far between. Again in 1982, Urney finished joint third from bottom in the league above Mountfield and Strabane. 1983 saw the club climb to fourth place in the League by mid-season, only to fall to 6th position.

Centenary year (1984) of the GAA brought little change to our league performance. In the Championship Urney drew with Windmill and defeated them in the reply on a score 1-08 to 0-05 before overcoming Loughmacrory in the quarter finals by 2-04 to 0-06. In the semi-final they met Clogher and for a change they showed true grit and determination as it took two replays to determine the winners. Goals from Kirk and Lafferty were not enough to take the lead with 2 minutes left, Clogher led by 2 points when sub Jim Hunter settled the game with Urney's third goal. Unfortunately the final against a very capable Pomeroy at Altnamuskin was totally one sided and they suffered a massive defeat by 19 points (0-02 to 3-12). It was a devastating result.

Things looked bleak for 1985 after this result but spirits were high and a firm purpose of amendment was high on the agenda at convention. It was decided to enter a reserve team in the League which was far from popular with many. The team proved their worth by winning the majority of their league matches and losing to Drumragh in Reserve Championship. On the back of the performance of the reserves the first team gained confidence and were lying in 3rd place after 12 games just one point from the top of the league. In the final game they hammered Strabane 6-10 to 0-07 with Billy McGhee scoring four goals.

The minors went one stage further defeating Moy in the semi-final 5-03 to 0-02 before losing to Kileshill; However silverware came to the village when St. Columba's Primary School won the North Tyrone Primary Schools Cup.

In the Junior Championship they defeated Drumquin in the semi-final by 0-09 to 0-08 and thus qualified to meet Drumragh in the final. Having caused upsets throughout the championship and having already defeated Drumragh in the League they were favourites to collect the title. Again, dreams were destroyed as Urney slumped to another miserable defeat 0-05 to 1-09.

Spirits in 1988 had not been hard to lift and this was shown in results having lost five games they qualified for a promotional play off but lost out to Eskra on a score of 0-07 to 1-09. In 1989 Strabane stopped their run of defeats by Urney when they won by 0-09 to 0-07 and Urney slaughtered Tattyreagh by 8-11 to 0-04 in the last game of the year. Sam Bogle was honoured as Tyrone Clubman of the Year at an event in the Burlington Hotel, Dublin and Paddy Corrigan became the second Urney referee to referee a Tyrone Snr Football Final. (Billy Melly refereed the 1966 final.) The first major event of 1990 was a concert to welcome Brian Farmer, President of the GAA in Canada and a leading industrialist who was a team mate of Gerry Convie, a native of Clonmore in Armagh and a then current player and official with Urney. The night was a huge success which lit the embers of rebirth as the next twenty years was to show.

Both on and off the pitch things developed and fell into place as Urney got things to succeed. They had a successful Jim Devlin Cup being unfortunate to lose to senior side Clonoe 2.10 to 1.10. In the league they crushed Tattyreagh 6-19 to 0-03, Aghaloo 2-12 to 2-06, beat Errigal Ciaran, In the Championship they had a huge win against Dregish in the preliminary round and against Tattyreagh in the first round of the championship. In the quarter final against Owen Roes where Jim Hunter converted a late 13 metre free to win the game. In the league, success continued against Derrytresk by 10 points. Meanwhile the reserve team remained undefeated in the league and progressed towards the final with Strabane before beating them in a replay. A first adult trophy since 1953 – a 31 year span.

In the Junior Final Urney played Aghaloo who were in their 2nd consecutive Final. Urney led at half time but looked a beaten side. It took all of Palor McNulty's experience to give them confidence to push on and win in the second half. Indeed, it took an outstanding save from Joe McCrory to awaken the Urney team. Urney pulled ahead as Aidan Langan made sure with a trademark goal. It was deemed to be one of the best Junior Finals seen in the county for many a day. Urney were not able to win the league having lost to Eskra one week after the Championship final. They finished runners up in the league.

1991 – 2010

It is hard to believe that in 1991 the club was trying to survive relegation back to Div 3. After much discussion it was decided that Urney should organise a huge fundraiser with £25,000 in prizes and £25,000 profit as part funding for future development - the reason for Brian Farmer's visit.

This year also brought great sadness to the club with the death of Urney's most consistent club member, Hugo Lafferty. He gave outstanding service to the club in terms of time, commitment, guidance and leadership. He was held in high esteem by all who knew him and equally held in fear by those who would have liked to put the boot into Urney especially at Board level.

The reserve team also won the league to go with the championship. Urney started well in the Intermediate grade and were League leaders at the half way stage. The fact that they only played one game in the next 2 months lost them their momentum. Almost everyone is aware of the "second birth "of the club during the last twenty years. The senior's team gained promotion to the senior league having won a playoff with Trillick. Trillick became the first team to lose a "play off" since the All County League was set up.

It was at this time that the club developed to become a fully organised unit with a mission. They set about developing a green field site that is now St Columba's Park with its clubrooms. This has cost in access of £500,000 and is debt free. Urney also won the Junior Championship in 2002 when they defeated Eskra on a score of 2-08 to 0-10.

Alongside this development a great energy has been put into getting quality coaching at all levels especially at youth levels. This has been obvious with the improved new skills provided by the coaches leading to several underage League and Championships titles, indeed this was especially true in 2010 when the U – 14 won league and championship titles, the U – 21 were unlucky not to reach the final and the senior's lost in the intermediate Championship final. The Ladies under 16 team lost both league and Championship finals.

Over the past number years much energy has been put into the Ladies football at underage level, where we now field teams at U8 - U10 - U12 - U14 - U16, U18 and in 2011 we will take part in the Ladies Adult League and Championship. An innovation in ladies football is "Gaelic for mother's" which has snowballed since being introduced in 2010.

Urney Senior Team Taken at Newtownstewart prior to their Division 2 promotion win over Greencastle. 2005 (Pic. Michael McGonagle)

Urney U16 Ladies Squad prior to league final against Loughmacrory, 2010.
Back row l-r , Shannen Mc Nulty , Caoilainn Kelly, Aine Conwell , Summer Kelly, Aoife Mc Menamin , Shannon Corry, Safan Lynch, Jennifer Leitch, Ellen Mc Gowan, Aimee Arnold, Maria Langan, Latoyah Moore, Lucy Arnold, Nicole Mc Daid, Tracy Kelly
Front row l-r, Rebecca Porter, Cliodhna Mc Menamin, Michaelina Mc Gonagle, Shannon Maxwell(C), Erin Campbell, Alanna Mc Bride, Lauren Casey, Aimee Mc Aleer, Gemma Conwell, Megan O'Neill

The Club can now look forward and plan for the future with boys teams at U8 - U10 - U12 - U14 - U16 - U18 - adult teams at U21 reserve and senior grade. This will entail substantial expenditure as we go in search for a new playing area, community centre and associated developments which are likely to cost the club £1,000,000 plus grants that may be available.

All in all it has been an adventure that has brought joy and sadness, in equal measures but it is the excitement of the future that makes us get involved. It is the voluntary nature of the GAA that makes the club the nucleus of the community. It is run by the community for the community and everyone is treated equal.

I have used "Urney: Portrait of an Irish Parish" written by Criostair Mac An Ultaigh - a past player and contributor to the betterment of Urney St Columba's.

Urney Senior Ladies prior to their first ever game. February 2011.
Front row l-r, Chanelle O'Donnell, Samantha Owens, Dympna Maxwell, Melissa Molloy, Collette Maxwell, Nadia Mc Ginley, Shannon Maxwell
Centre l-r, Donna Lafferty, Claire Mc Cauley, Kim Graham, Latoyah Moore, Ciara Millar, Orlagh O'Neill
Back row l-r, Angie Porter, Catherine Mc Granaghan, Denise Mc Crory, Grainne Bogle, Karina Mc Sorley, Claire Foley, Lisa Mc Ginley, Lisa Mc Donald, kirsty Potts, Margaret Mc Bride, Cora Bogle, kathy Mc Menamin, Michella Mc Sorley, Maria Langan

Football
TYRONE AND DONEGAL UNITED FOOTBALL LEAGUE

HOLMES CUP- FINAL TIE.
Clady Strollers v. Convent Court, Strabane.

Three teams met on Saturday, in the Recreation Park, Strabane, in the final for the above competition, before a large gathering of spectators. The Strollers, having won the toss, elected to play with the wind. Logue kicked off for the Court, but the Strollers forwards, getting procession by a nice bit of combination, beat the Court custodian scarcely half a minute from the start. The Strollers still continued to press and forced a corner, which M'Grath placed nicely and Lennon headed through, giving the Strollers their second goal. The Court livened up and kept the ball in the visitor's territory for some time, but White-in goal- was equal to the occasion, saving some very dangerous shots. At length Carlin let his forwards away by a long drive, and the Strollers got another corner, which Sheerin cleared, but Gallen getting procession scored the third goal. The Strollers still continued to press, and Lennon sent in a high shot which, apparently, went under the bar, but the referee thought otherwise, and at half-time the score stood : - Strollers, 3 goals; Convent Court, nil. With the wind in their favour in the second half the Court began to make matters lively, but Carlin and Taylor at back kept the forwards at bay. At length Calvert beat White with a shot, close in. This seemed to encourage the Court and for a long time they kept up the pressure and were awarded a penalty, which Gibbons drove through.

The game now became very exciting, both sides trying hard to increase their score; the Strollers having the best of the play, but were very unlucky about goals- some good chances were missed for want of coolness. The Strollers were pressing hard when the whistle sounded, leaving the score –Strollers, 3 Court, 2. For the winners Carlin and Taylor at back did splendid. White and Gallen were the best of the halves, the forwards all played well, M'Grath, Lennon, and Creanor were the best. Logue, Calvert, Griffin, Donnell, and Mullen showed up well for the losers.

The following were the teams: -Clady Strollers—Goal, White ; backs, Carlin and Taylor ; halves, Gallagher, Gallen, M'Grath ; forwards, K. M'Grath, J. M'Grath, Lennon, M'Kinney, and Creanor. Convent Court—Goal, M'Menamin ; backs, Mullin and Sheerin; halves, Harte, O'Neill, Griffin ; forwards, Donnell, Gibbons, Logue, Lafferty, Calvert, Mr. F. Reynolds, Sion Mills, was referee and gave entire infection. (Taken from Strabane Chronicle 1899)

Clady Strollers

DONEYLOOP YOUTH CLUB

By Brid McGrenra

Doneyloop Youth Club was set up in 2005 when our now Club President, Mack McLaughlin saw the need for a social / recreational outlet for the young people of the area. He approached Charlie Byrne of Drumdoit and John McGrenra of Alt Lower and asked if they would be interested in forming a Youth Club and both agreed. Thereafter followed a series of meetings with Louise McBride, Youth Worker with Donegal Youth Service, Letterkenny and a Committee was formed. The Club was then affiliated to Donegal Youth Service who provided Youth Leadership and Child Protection training for our first Youth Leaders, Charlie Byrne, Fiona Byrne, John McGrenra and Shauna Kirk.

Further youth leadership training followed and a larger number of volunteers were trained, i.e., Helen Collins, Loretta McNulty, Brid McGrenra, Neil Gallagher, Damian Wright, Daniel McMenamin, Breda McConnell, Rita Wright, Paddy Bell, Alison Bell, John Byrne, Patsy McElchar, Tina Lafferty, Debbie Mc Nulty, Brendan Morris, Ann Marie Crawford, Celia Byrne and Karen Guthrie. Between 2007/2008 further leaders came on board, namely, Emma McMenamin, Simon McMenamin, Jason Harold, Noel Burns, Matthew Harold, Elaine Byrne, John O'Donnell, Josephine McElchar, Valerie Bradley, Alan James, Pauric Bell and Aisling Bell.

Doneyloop Youth Club trip to Belfast, June 2006.

With the Youth Club based in the Community Centre where it shared the use of the main hall with other groups within the community, it was decided to erect a purpose built building solely for youth club use. Permission was sought from Fr. Brian McGoldrick, PP., who supported the venture from the beginning and a 35 year Lease was sought and obtained from the Derry Diocesan Trust chaired by Bishop Seamus Hegarty. Grant aid for the building and contents was received from Donegal Local Development Company through Leader and Clar; the National Lottery; Department of Health and Children; Donegal County Council, VEC; Castlefin/Lifford Community Health Forum; the HSE and the Department of Community, Rural and Gaeltacht Affairs. The Club now offers to young people a fully equipped Club Room and to the community, a fully equipped gym which offers annual or pay-as-you-go membership; spinning classes; yoga and aerobics.

The installation of a computer suite is now complete in our new facility which offers to the youth of our area a facility for after school learning, i.e., homework class; computer classes; safe internet use and many more "up-to-date" "cool" experiences on computers.

Doneyloop Youth Club has also secured funding through Donegal County Council's Peace III Programme managed by the Special EU Programmes Body. Not only has this Peace III grant provided funding for the research and publication of this book, it has also enabled the Club to provide a community sensory garden, the erection of bilingual signs for each townland on the Doneyloop side of the parish, cross border intergenerational outings and youth club cultural / recreational trips The funding has also given the Club an unique opportunity to work with other Cross Border Youth Clubs on projects on equality, diversity and culture.

At present the Club has 95 members that are divided between the Junior club and the Senior club. The Clubs run two evenings per week at the moment and attendance is high in both clubs indicating that there is a strong interest from all members.

Activities include indoor ball sports, indoor net games, personal development courses, talent/variety show competitions, darts, air hockey, cookery, pool, snooker, wi-fi games, quizzes, arts and crafts and a variety of fun floor games. We also run several day trips throughout the year, which include water based pursuits, ice skating, team building and educational trips to Glenveagh National Park, Ulster American Folk Park, W5 Science Museum, Belfast and cross border field events with other Clubs, e.g., Castlederg Community Art Forum.

The Club has won the Youth Club of the year for the years 2007, 2008 and 2009 from Donegal Youth Service with children from the Club representing the North-West area in the Youth Work Ireland games in Limerick in 2008 and 2009. Also success has being gained at All Ireland level in the national variety show competitions. The teenagers in the Senior Club have completed both level 1 and level 2 Personal Development Accredited Courses, First Aid Courses and three members have completed Child Protection Courses.

The club is financed on an ongoing basis by the small entrance fee that members pay on attendance each evening and the finance generated from classes held and from gym membership. This money goes towards maintenance and running costs and is used to subsidise the cost of more expensive day trips and tours. Other monies raised annually have been through fundraising, e.g., a 5 mile sponsored walk, sponsored Dublin City Marathon run, private donations, Christmas bazaar, car boot sale and a fashion show.

This new facility has greatly added to the social/recreational/educational life of the youth, elderly and the socially disadvantaged of our rural isolated area. With hard work and determination, Doneyloop Youth Club has a duty to offer it's young people and the wider community, who have always been deprived of any social / recreational outlet, the best support that can be obtained. Therefore, having the right sponsorship, parental support and advice is imperative to the continued success of this very rural Club. Recognition must be given to all the youth leaders and volunteers who run the club week after week, year after year on a voluntary basis.

Yesterday is History – Tomorrow a Mystery – Today a Present

THE BEGINNING. Doneyloop Youth Club 2005.

Michael (Mac) McLaughlin

Michael (Mac) McLaughlin was born in Drumnaha in 1936 in the house in which he still lives. His father James Patrick (J.P.) was born in 1892 also in the same house and his mother Catherine Mc Monagle was born just across the road in 1901. They were both into drama which was big in the Clady area at the time, an art not carried on by Mac. They both went to old Alt school and when his father left school, he travelled the world with the merchant navy. Mac states that his father must have had a good standard of education as anything he did was never up to his father's standard. When his mother left school she worked in Urney Chocolate factory, going to Scotland when the factory closed.

Mac was born with 'club feet' and his father brought him to Belfast to see specialists from England 33 times in three years costing 100 guineas a time. Mac was told by a neighbour "don't forget your father made himself a poor man trying to put your feet right." A trip to Dublin and surgery got him back on his feet and Mac believes the medical staff in Dublin were as good a match if not better than their English counterparts at the time.

He remembers his mother taking down bacon that was hanging from the kitchen ceiling, cutting a piece of it for dinner and hanging the rest up for another day. There was always a plentiful supply of eggs, cabbage, milk and butter and although money was scarce, he never remembers going hungry. His father did not believe in smuggling but made an exception with turkeys which he would fatten up for sale at Christmas. The turkeys were carried from his house in Drumnaha, through Mc Pherson's lane, over a wooden footbridge across the burn and in past John Hanna's farm, not an easy task as a nine year old carrying a twenty five pound live turkey.

There were two teachers in Alt when Mac was at school, Mrs Linsday and Miss Mc Kenna from Dungiven. Miss Mc Kenna's sister had a shop in Castlefinn. Gaelic football was the big sport in school at the time with the likes of Paddy Rushe, Seamus Crawford and Gerry Mc Croary all hoping to be the next Phil 'the gunner' Brady of the great Cavan team. Mac left primary school at fourteen and spent three years at the Technical school in Stranorlar. Mac was sent to the Finn College but wanting to do woodwork went himself to the Tech. His parents did not find out until the end of the first year. Mac's job in the morning was to bring the cattle down to a field in Doneyloop when going to school and bring them back home in the evening.

After leaving school, Mac took a job with Donegal County Council as a Clarke of Works for four years. He then decided to go to teaching college in Gorey, Co Wexford where he spent three years. His first job was in Leitrim where because the school was ready to close, he was asked to be acting principal. After that he spent three years in Carrygallen, Leitrim (one as Vice Principal) before coming back as Principal to Buncranna in 1972. After eight years and finding it hard to both teach in Buncrana and farm at home, Mac "demoted himself" to get back to Stranorlar. Mac retired in 2001, after 35 years teaching.

Over the years Mac has been involved in many voluntary community organisations. He was a founder member of the Castlefinn Social Services, St Bridget's Football and Camogie clubs and Finn Valley Sheepdog Association while also playing a leading role in various parish councils, school parents committee's to name but a few and in 2005 became the first honorary President of Doneyloop Youth Club.

Mac at a prize giving ceremony for a computer class held in Doneyloop Youth Club.

Christina Speers

Christina Speers was born in Carrickone Urney in 1920. Her father John Hall came from near Ballinadrait while her mother Martha (nee Gibson) came from Ardstraw. Christina remembers the work on the farm when she was growing up. "We had to get up in the morning and go for the cows. The mornings were magnificent once we got outside and felt the dewy morning air – it was so fresh. The country was clear and cool – the smoke ascending from the neighbouring chimneys across the field." All fires had to be lit to boil a kettle and cook breakfast. Gas and electricity were unknown in those days." Christina was often up by six thirty but was never asked to milk the cows; milking was not one of her strong points

She remembers her mother baking soda bread and delightful treacle scones. "A bread man selling loaf bread and special fruit loaves, each containing a ring at Halloween, came round every Tuesday and Friday on a horse drawn cart. Bob Hamilton from Clady came around on a Friday selling groceries. Every second Wednesday there was a van from Colhoun's of Main Street, Strabane which brought the weekly necessities, bacon came in pound parcels wrapped in greaseproof paper and we sold our eggs to them. The egg money helped pay for the goods." Christina and her sisters used to help churn the milk to make butter "My Mother then washed the butter with cold water and shaped it into blocks or circles. If she made it into a circle, she had a special wooden print of a thistle which she pressed on top of the butter; you could easily see when the butter was set"

Christina went to Urney Public Elementary School where the pupils sat at long desks with five children to each desk."When we were given our spellings, we stood back to back and the teacher called out our spellings and we would write down the answers on our jotters. For geography, we stood around maps which were hanging on the wall. These were lowered and we pointed out various places but we talked more to ourselves than we did about the map". For games out in the playground, Christina and her friends played tig, and "my sheep lie low" which was similar to "hide and seek". Boys played football and the girls bounced balls against the walls,

Following on from primary school Christina went to the Convent of Mercy Secondary School in Strabane. She would cycle in and out of Strabane every day in all weathers.

Christina trained at Stranmillis College as a school teacher from 1939 to 1941. Due to the war the college was evacuated from Belfast to Fawcett's Hotel in Portrush. Her first teaching experience was as a substitute in Lisnaskea for a fortnight, followed by a few months in Castlederg. She then taught at Castlemellon School outside Donemana as a substitute for Mr Moorehead who had joined the Army. This school had a problem with rats and Christina every morning before going in, shook the door to frighten the unwelcome creatures. She taught for a period in Sion Mills before being appointed Principal at Tullywhisher in 1945 where she remained until retirement.

She remembers the day the war ended "We went into Strabane in the evening and danced in the street where the old Post Office is now, to music relayed from McCurdy's shop. Then we went on to a Service of Thanksgiving in Strabane Presbyterian Church. On Smuggling Christina had this to say "People smuggled sugar from McEvoys shop at Cloghfin and smuggled tea in a different direction from the North into the Republic where it was very scarce and could cost £1 per pound in Dublin – a lot of money then. Rationing was part of life because clothes coupons were necessary to purchase garments, but at McGinty's in Ballybofey everything was available. A waterproof coat purchased there was confiscated by the Customs before crossing at Clady, but was returned on payment of a fine. A lot depended on the customs man on duty at Clady. We brought skeins of wool hanging as a scarf around our necks, but concealed by the upturned collar of our coats.

Christina retired in 1981 and lives in Bellspark. She has given many years service to the church in Urney and has served on numerous committees and helped with many fund raising activities.

Joe Mc Devitt

Joe Mc Devitt was born in Inchenny in 1935 and has grown up with a great sense and love of history especially local history. He went to school in Barrack Street School in Strabane as some of his aunts worked in a factory in the town. He remembers as a young boy taking the "wee Donegal" on trips from Clady to Ballybofey. "The railcars were very comfortable. They would stop anywhere for you. I remember them stopping to pick up mass goers on a Sunday morning. One of the train drivers was Marty Harron. When the farmers were out in the field they used the train as a watch, when the train would pass, they knew it was time for dinner"

The border did not affect Joe when he was growing up as there were no crossing points near Inchenny. Joe partook in a bit of smuggling in his time, cigarettes which were cheaper in the South were taken across the border by Joe and his friends but they had to watch out for the water guards or the "water rats" as they were called.

Joe has many historic documents in connection with flax mills in Urney. His Grandfather had two mills, one in Clady and one in Inchenny. He "laments the loss of so many important documents held onto by the older generation but thrown away by the younger generation who believe they are not of historical importance".

Joe believes the time of the hiring fair was a black time in our history with young boys and girls sent out to do "slave labour". He tells the story of one young boy from Donegal hired to a farm in Inchenny who had to eat all his meals out in a shed.

The wakes and funerals of yesteryear" were more like a concert with tea and cigarettes going around as if there was no tomorrow!" He does not remember drink ever being served at wakes in the area. The weddings were a more modest affair than we have today. "A wedding would take place in early morning with a meal laid on in one of the houses for the afternoon". Only the two families would be invited to the big day Joe remembers.

The Carricklee races was a great day out with people travelling from near and far, "people would come from Convoy, Ballybofey and as far away as Derry".

Electricity did not come to Inchenny until around 1975. Joe tells of going through Barnesmore on the train wondering how electricity could have reached "the middle of nowhere" while they were in darkness two miles from Strabane. "Phones were in some houses before the power".

In his young day, Joe's house was always full of visitors calling around for a chat, and it is a testament to the man that is Joe Mc Devitt, that his home is still a stronghold for visitors in 2011.

Early morning wedding (9A.M.) of John Joe Mc Menamin and Mary Jane Doherty with best man Joe Mc Menamin and Bridesmaid Annie Mc Girr (nee Doherty), followed by breakfast at home.

Locals with visitors from Scotland.
Front L-R: ? , ? , ? , Francis Haughey, Patsy Casey,
Middle: Biddy Gallagher, ? , Eleen Wray, Nellie Fee,
Back: Charlie Haughey, Tessie Haughey, Helena Houston, Flora Fee, Anne Kirk, Jimmy Houston, Jimmy Kilpatrick.

Included in this group are—Mr. and Mrs. Reid, Miss Margaret Schooner, Mrs. Duffy, Mrs. Bogle, Mrs. Harper, Mi Gallen, John Martin, Mrs. Martin, Mrs. Maxwell, Alec Darragh, Eddie Forester, John Burns, Miss Mary Nelis,Fra Canning, Mrs. McCorkell, Mrs. Corry, Mrs. Haire and Miss B. Gallen.

Cross- broder group

Urney - History / People / Place

And Mary got the blame

By Jane Domitric (Mc Corkell)

It's hard to imagine a time when spending hours watching television and playing video games was not our main source of recreation, but in the early 1950's most of us never even imagined such pastimes. However, we were able to find much more exciting ways to pass the few free hours we had in activities that might be considered delinquent by today's standards.

In the 1950's my family came to live with my grandfather in Clady, a small village where all the residents knew everyone and their families. The village had two pubs, two shops, a forge, a scutch mill and a two-room school. As there were no organized sports for children and little opportunity to get to activities outside the village, children found or made their own entertainment.

Warnings to stay away from water, fire and other equally ominous dangers were given constantly but not always heeded. Most times, the news of an unsuspecting child's misdeeds reached home before he did and he would often be met by irate parents prepared to dole out the appropriate punishment even if he thought he could explain himself and more often before he could explain.

So in the autumn evenings when it got dark early, the sport of lighting bonfires would begin down the back hill and in the empty lot known as the wall steads. At first the small bonfires seemed exciting enough. Then the bigger and more daring kids would go down to the scutch mill at the bottom of the village to fill bags with shows and bring them up to pour on the fires and soon the fires would be shooting red and orange flames high in the air and bright sparks would seem to light up the night sky. To a small child it was like fireworks on a special occasion like America's Fourth of July. My mother warned us to stay away and we promised we would but it was impossible to stay away when the whole world seemed to be there having a grand time. Of course we lied about being even near the fires. At the time I was about five or six years old and my sister not much older.

One evening we returned home and were surprised by my mother's extreme anger that we had disobeyed her. We couldn't understand how she caught us out. Alas, I, being of little brain, had sat on a stone which somehow burned a hole in my skirt. Perhaps sparks from the fiery shows had landed on the stone where I sat. My sister had suffered a pair of singed eyebrows and both of us smelled of smoke. Being the youngest, I got off with a scolding but my sister, then and on later occasions, was given a good hiding for leading me astray. Justifiably, she hated me for a long time after that and she and her friends never wanted to take me on other adventures such as going from house to house putting on little plays, knocking on doors and running away, and swimming in the glen not to mention attending wakes unaccompanied by adults. Who needed a television or an electronic game?

Shopping in Alt.

By Daniel Crawford

Thomas and Rose Crawford who got married in the thirties decided to open a shop where they resided in Alt. It mainly consisted of groceries and farm produce. A lot of the goods came from Dublin by Rail via Castlefin. Tea, sugar, flour and maize were packed in tea chests and eight stone packs.

They had to be weighed by hand into ¼lbs and ½lbs bags. Maize and flour were bagged in 7 and 14lbs. As the family came along they one by one had to do their share of working and serving in the shop. It was a very busy shop as it stood at the border, so therefore they had both North and South customers.

They came from as far away as Sionmills, Newtonstewart, Spamount and Castlederg. As time went on Thomas started a mobile shop which was drawn by horse and float. He covered a wide area of Castlefin, summer and winter which in those days the weather was very harsh. In the fifties they opened a second shop at Alt Upper three miles from Castlederg.

It was after the war years, so food was very scarce and dear in Northern Ireland and also rationed so it helped the border areas quite a lot. Thomas and Rose returned to live in Cormakilly in the sixties after a very happy and successful thirty years of business.

Taking the Tea

By Bernie Mc Corkell

I remember two scutch mills in Clady. Hamilton's mill nearest where we lived in the "gavels" was out of commission as far as I can recall but the building and the water wheel were still standing for a number of years after this. At the time the street was known as Mill Street. The water to drive the wheel came from the dam field. (*New Street and the Crescent housing estates are now on this site.*) It flowed from there under the road at Mill Street as far as a nice concreted area before hitting the wheel. In the summer we would sit on the concrete ledge and dangle our feet in the water splashing it over each other. We also climbed on to the wheel and tried to move it only to be chased away by Aunt Cassie who was never too far away.

The other mill which was owned by John O Flaherty provided much work for the people in Clady and surrounding areas. Our job after school was to take tea to friends and family in tin cans. The men came out of the mill covered in dust head to toe and sat in the big shed where the tow was piled up to have a well earned break and enjoy the tea.

We used to play and jump about in the beautiful, white, silky tow even though we weren't allowed to but the boss never caught us. Soon the wheel started up again and the men went back to work in the mill. Some of us stayed a while and peeped in to see the wipers stripping the dried lint to make it into tow. The bits that fell on to the floor were called shows. These were gathered up and collected by the villagers to use as fuel for the fire. Because of this we were called the *Clady show shakers* by people from outside the village.

I loved taking the tea to the workers. On a Saturday I got 2 shillings and sixpence from Frank Nelis. However I got nothing from Jim because he is my brother.

The Show Fire

By Mary Mc Corkell

The waste material from Flax after it was rolled was called 'shows'. I remember the first time I saw a show fire. It was in my grandfather's house in the main street in Clady. We lived in Sion Mills at the time and visited on Sundays. It was a bright orangey red color all over and gave off an intense heat. Apparently show fires were dusty and smelly but I don't remember that and anyhow there were no carpets or grand furniture to protect.

There was a knack in building a fire with shows. Two long pieces of cylindrical wood called kiln sticks were used to create a draught, one placed in the centre of the hearth floor front to back, the other standing upright at the inner end of the first piece near the back of the hearth. Some people used two bottles. The shows were piled up on top of the wood and patted firmly down. The wood was carefully pulled out creating a funnel to make the draught and a light was put in the central space. When it was fully lit it could burn for hours. Burning was prolonged by damping the shows. Most of the people in the village made fires from shows. It was free and an effective method of heating and cooking if you had an open hearth as most houses had back then. The shows were stored in a shed beside the mill and available to all who wanted them. Mary Rose Mc Ginley said she and her friend brought a hand cart with them from Ballylast down the Lifford road to the mill in Clady for shows. The lads called after them "Put your head down and pull like a donkey"

My grandfather used to scutch in a mill in Donegal near Castlefinn. It was called Portsallagh mill about two miles from Clady over the border in Co Donegal. There is no trace of a mill there now but there is evidence of a stream. My mother talked of her embarrassment at having to walk the donkey down Clady Street over the bridge to the mill when she was a young girl. I used to wonder why a donkey was needed to take his lunch and tea. Very likely it was to bring bales of shows back to the house to burn. I don't know and didn't think to ask.

Forts and Fairies

By John Byrne

The Fort at Drumdoit

As a young boy playing and working on my father's farm (Charlie Byrne) at Drumdoit, little did I realise the full history of the different forts, rocks and wells in the locality. You always knew that there was something special there, for example the old fort is on one of my Dad's fields, he called it the Fairy Fort and I remember maybe not so long-ago mid-seventies gathering potatoes in this field and wondering as a little boy 'do leprechauns live in the fort, where do they hide and what do they do?' Some of these forts date as far back as the time of our Lord. There was certainly a feeling of something very special there. The whole valley would have been covered in dense woodland with wild animals roaming around with battling tribes nearby, battling for survival. This was their safe haven for their family, animals and food, a round high flat mound of clay. They did not have the modern comforts that we have and take for granted such as comfortable homes with electricity, lights, televisions, computers, water taps, Schools, Doctors, supermarkets, cars, Etc.

The Grey Stone Home at Drumdoit

St. Safan's National School is built on a field that was once referred to as 'The Grey Stone Home'. A large Grey Stone stood in this field hence the name 'The Grey Stone Home'. The stone was buried years ago beside the school. The top of the stone can still be seen coming through the soil. As children we used to play around it and climb over and on top of this big bolder. It must have been over 5ft high and 6ft wide. We were told of the battle of the giants, Finn Mac Cool and a Scottish giant, and how Finn had thrown this rock at the Scottish Giant. Even Finn's hand mark was still on the rock, though as I recall it took some searching to find it. But nowadays they would lead you to believe that an Ice glazier would have left it there after the Ice age. Well I favour the giant's story myself. Hopefully someday this piece of history / mythology will be seen again.

Old Country Shops

There was lots of little shops in the countryside in the mid-nineteen hundreds, old Tommie Crawford had a shop at the border and at Alt Upper Jack & Nuala Foley had a shop beside the church and the school at Upper Alt. There was a shop across the road from where St. Safan's School is now, and there was Canning's old shop at Doneyloop by the chapel. Brown's had a shop at Ringsend, to name a few that I know of. These shops were a very humble affair, no fridge freezers and were very small. Meats were covered in salt and cloth sometimes lying on the floor at your feet. There was no such thing as a sell by date when these shops were around. Your nose was the only way of knowing what was fit to be eaten and what was fit for the dogs.

Mr and Mrs Thomas Crawford who owned a shop beside their house in Alt Upper.

BIBLIOGRAPHY

BARTLETT.T and JEFFERY.K (ed) 'A Military History of Ireland' (1996)
Blair May, 'Hiring fairs and market places' (Appletree Press Ltd 2007)
Bloodstock Breeders Review, (1924)
Bradley Jim, 'The fair river valley' (Ulster Historical Foundation 2000)
CAHILL .T, 'How the Irish saved Civilization' (Anchor Books, NY, 1996)
Canon D.W.T. Crooks, 'Living Stones – A Survey of the Churches of the Dioceses of Derry and Raphoe' (Styletype Printing Ltd, Glengormley 2001)
Canon G.J.A. Carson 'In His Hand 1870 – 1970'
Canon J.B. Leslie, 'Clergy of Derry' (1937) edited and updated by Canon D.W.T. Crooks and Canon F.W. Fawcett, (Ulster Historical Foundation, 1999)
Carlin W.J. 'THE EPIC OF MASTER ROBERT' as told by Tom Patton.
County Donegal presentments (assizes)
County Tyrone Assizes
Curtis, E 'History of Ireland' (1922)
Dónall Mac Giolla Easpaig Ma, The Placenames Commission, Department for Community, Equality and Gaeltacht Affairs
Donegal archives, Lifford
Donegal Democrat.
Donegal Peoples press.
DONNELLY, TP (Father) 'A History of the Parish of Ardstraw West and Castlederg' (Mourne Art Printing, STRABANE, 1978)
Dr Kay Muhr, Northern Ireland Place-Name Project, Queen's University Belfast
Gage Conolly, Manor of Castlefinn, Map book (1816)
Gailey Alan, 'Rural housing in mid-nineteenth century Ulster' (H.M.S.O 1974)
GANTZ.J 'Early Irish Myths and Sagas' (PENGUIN BOOKS, LONDON, 1981)
GEBBIE, JOHN H.[ED.] 'An Introduction to the Abercorn Letters' (Strule press Omagh 1972)
Grey Toney, 'Saint Patrick's People' (Little, Brown and Company, 1996)
Haire William and Maxwell Craig, 'Life And Times Of Urney Presbyterian Church' (Urney Presbyterian Church 2005)
Harte Paddy, 'County Donegal Book of Honour. The Great War 1914-1918'
Harte Paddy, 'The Island of Ireland Peace Park and the First World War'
Hayden Tom, 'Irish Hunger' (Roberts Rinehart 1998)
Hearth money roll, Urney, Tyrone. (1666)
Historical notes of Raphoe, Finn Valley, Lifford and Twin Towns
Irish Folklore Commission, 1936/37.
JEFFERIES, H.A. and DEVLIN, C/(ed) 'History of the Diocese of Derry' (FOUR COURTS PRESS, DUBLIN 2000)
Joyce P.W. 'Irish names of places' (1873)